IOAOM

Insights of an Ordinary Man

WAYNE ALLEN LEVINE

Spirit
Wind
BOOKS

Spirit Wind
B O O K S

Spirit Wind Books,
an Imprint of
Love Your Life Publishing
7127 Mexico Road Suite 121
St. Peters, MO 63346
www.loveyourlifepublishing.com

ISBN: 978-1-934509-90-6

Library of Congress Control Number: 2011940418
Printed in the United States of America
Second Printing 2016

Cover and internal design: www.Cyanotype.ca
Editing by Gwen Hoffnagle
Author Photo: Luke Wooden

Contents

✳   ✳   ✳

Introduction

✳   ✳   ✳

In a certain well-imagined sense, I feel as if this book began as soulful graffiti scribbled onto the walls of my mother's womb, with my newly formed fingers repeatedly dipped into disappearing amniotic ink. In other words, I feel as if I've been writing this book from the very beginning. But let me start with yesterday and leap both forward and backward from there.

Part of my yesterday involved the quixotic joy of chasing luminous clouds along the landscape of my life. My great mid-day excursion was up the steepest hill behind my house, then down again. It's all about stealing moments – or borrowing instances that can't be stolen because they're offered freely to those who seize the time and opportunity to claim them. The best we can do a good part of the time is to give our fullest attention to the fleeting – to pay homage to the quixotic and give our sincere praise to the capricious – chasing clouds, pruning roses and/or other flowers, planting trees, writing poetry, singing love songs, watering an immaculate garden, or building monuments for future generations to reflect on.

What really lasts? What remains of all our thoughts and efforts? What, more than anything else, do we hope and pray and wish with all our hearts to always remember? And what do we – above all else – wish to be remembered for? What is the yearning, burning, ecstatic heartache that lifts us up and lets us down intermittently? These are among the meaningful questions that follow us through our everyday, attempting to guide and inspire us whether we are aware of it or not. We keep coming back to those soul-shaping questions whether we care to or not, because those are the questions that refuse to let us go!

We are the clouds and dreams we continue to chase. We are the tender pink quixotic petals glowing momentarily on all the fertile branches of those seasonal plum trees. And we might also be related in spirit to the giant pines and deep-rooted redwoods that live for over a thousand years, giving oxygen to those of us who keep coming back to the meaningful and sometimes haunting questions that help shape and guide our lives.

The body and soul of this book has been guided, as much as anything, by these questions. Fate and destiny are the recurring themes, along with my artful attempt to distinguish the subtle difference between the two in order to honor the creative energy that unites them. Destiny is what we choose to do with the fate we've been given. That's the primary distinction I make from day to day. Knowing what we think and sense and act upon does, indeed, make all the difference.

Fate, destiny, and my unbridled love and passion for the creative process – those three things, inextricably woven into the fabric of life, create the central thesis of this book you're about to venture into – the thesis for which there is no longer any antithesis that tempts me to reconsider what I know I'm meant to do.

The chronology of any long-term creative endeavor is often compelling enough to encourage an author, artist, or spirited architect to offer detailed charts and colorful maps, allowing us to follow their trajectory within our own awareness. This introduction is in the vein of such an attempt. I wrestled with the urge to write the entire book you're now holding within the body of this basic introduction, in order to acquaint you with it and hopefully make you feel eager to leap into it. The book itself – through honest stories, heartfelt vignettes, timeless reflections, and scattered poems, will best reveal the trajectory of this life I've been given and am honored to share with you. This is my impassioned invitation to you to keep reading – to turn the pages and tap in to the beauty, power, and energy of your own unique awareness.

These are simply the insights of an ordinary man – IOAOM – with its acronymic Os for eyes looking up at you as you glance over them, and when those Os for eyes close or disappear, we are then left only with "I AM."

What Will You Do if You Don't Win the Lottery?

❋   ❋   ❋

What will you do if you don't win the lottery? That's a question we tend not to ask ourselves or pose to others. And why should we? Where's the fun and excitement in a question like that? How can we be expected to locate our dreams and make our lengthy list of extravagant things we intend to buy if and when our quick-pick or psychically selected numbers turn over and make us into instant millionaires?

And that is precisely why we need to ask – not what we'll buy if we win, but what we plan to do if we don't. Because what we do is what matters; our actions are always the deciding and defining factors in our lives. Shakespeare said, "Action is eloquence," and Goethe told us to "be bold and the mighty forces will come to our aid." Descartes should have said, "I act, therefore I am," but apparently failed to. We may proclaim that we exist because we think, ponder, and continue to fantasize about the always and forever better life, but thought without action – when action is needed – tends to be little more than an intellectual exercise in futility. Thinking without acting rarely, if ever, leads us to any deep sense of fulfillment. Of course, the opposite approach – acting without thinking – tends to produce dangerously unfavorable results for many people.

I didn't intend to turn this into a philosophical treatise about buying lottery tickets; however, I am a philosopher, as well as a poet, and so what else could it be? And now the question has become: To buy or not to buy a lottery ticket? This is one of the questions I answered for myself more than a decade ago. There is a fundamental difference between being and buying which I intend to explore in this brief essay (or bold vignette, depending upon its length and your perception).

Eleven years ago I was struggling to maintain a life of mediocrity – doing my damnedest to try to fit in where I really didn't belong. There is nothing rare or exceptional about a situation like that; in fact, most of the people I know are living their own version of it. Having been there myself, I remain sensitive to the struggle to get out of such a situation when we know in our hearts and souls that we truly need to. I was there long enough to have earned the insights that I wish now to share with those who may want to make use of them. And I don't have to think very long or look very far to realize there are plenty of you.

More and more people are working longer and harder for less than what they were earning a decade ago (when we adjust for the rate of inflation), driven by a deeply misguided bottom-line mindset, fueled by fear, and shaped by greed as much as anything. There are plenty of facts, figures, and statistical data to support the opinions, beliefs, and faulty notions on all sides. The numbers are widely available elsewhere – in other books, printed reports, newspapers, and in both print and online magazines – but not here. I prefer to speak from my own area of expertise, which is philosophy and the poetry that emerges from my personal experience. I am, after all, the world's foremost expert on my very own personal experience, and I will continue to draw from that.

I bought my last lottery ticket eleven years ago while attempting to figure out how to extricate myself from the work routine, which at that time was less than to my liking. I was searching for a way out – a healthy way in which to make a legitimate and significant change. It wasn't as if things were really awful in my life; in fact, there were a number of things that I thought to be wonderful back then, and still do to this day. Still and all, there was something deeply fundamental to my being that was missing. When we are less than satisfied with our daily routine, there is a tendency to believe we can buy our way out of it and spend our way into a better one, which is not entirely true nor entirely false. When we sense that something deep is missing, the thing we need and want the most isn't something we can purchase, even if we choose the winning lotto numbers, making us into instant multi-millionaires.

So did I have the winning ticket with a $40,000,000 payday? Did my numbers line up eleven years ago, permitting me to make the change I felt the need to make? I won't say yet. I'll let you wonder; I'll allow you to guess for now, though I promise to tell you before the end of this vignette.

There I was, holding that little ticket in my hand, wondering what I would do if I won. Where would I want to live if I could afford to live nearly anywhere? What kind of car (or cars!) would I buy? How much would I spend on fine art to hang on the many walls of the numerous rooms of my new home? And once I had my new home filled with fine antiques and masterful art to ponder freely and appreciate fully, and my shiny new cars, and a thousand or more artfully-bound first edition books, arranged by subject, filling the custom-made mahogany shelves in my exquisite home library – and the list could go on and on ad infinitum

– what to do? No matter what we have or don't have, what to *do* remains the real core question we keep coming back to.

What did I really want to do? When your imagination seems to be in suspended animation and your creative mind has been sentenced to solitary confinement, surrounded by the noise of screaming prisoners, thinking about the things you might do if you did win the lottery can be a useful trick to loosen the lock on the cell that you've put yourself in. Once I felt free enough to imagine some of the things I would acquire if I could afford them, the restraints I had placed upon an array of bold and bright possibilities began to vanish with the afternoon wind. I knew what I wanted to do, what I needed to do, and what I was determined to do no matter what! I wanted to write. I needed to write. And I would write if the numbers lined up or if they didn't. Win or lose, the answer was the same: "I am a writer, and I will write."

And once again, with that lottery ticket still in my hand, I felt compelled to ask myself, "What will I do if I don't win the lottery?" And now that I knew, it was rather easy for me to answer. Then I asked myself these questions: "Do I really want to win? In my heart of hearts, do I sincerely hope to be holding the winning ticket? Do I really want to join the ranks of instant lottery winners?" And my true and honest answer – mano a mano – was: "No. I would much prefer to earn my fortune as a direct result of my full commitment to the work I was destined to do."

I didn't want to win something that could possibly rob me of the need to fulfill my fate. I didn't want to be given anything that could lessen my desire to dig deeply enough to discover my own understanding. And as I say that now, I can hear the masses chanting in unison, "The hell with understanding! Just give me the $40,000,000."

I could easily understand such a chant, and at another time I might have been tempted to join in. But on that memorable day eleven years ago, when I asked myself in earnest if I really wanted to win the lottery, my answer that day was: "No. I really don't." And I've been winning nearly every single solitary day ever since!

I am a winner each and every morning when I wake with gratitude and eagerness to continue. I leap out of bed – literally from the foot of my bed – directly into the day before me. I leap forward with a rich, unbridled sense of enthusiasm to carry on with the work I love in this life that I've been given. "One learns by doing a thing; for though you think you know it, you have no certainty until you try." That is something Sophocles said in about 440 BCE, and it remains relevant to this day.

So was I a winner that fated day eleven years ago? Yes! I most certainly was. Did the numbers on my lottery ticket all line up in order to make me an instant multi-millionaire? No, they did not. Am I doing what I love and living true to my understanding? Yes, I am; absolutely, without a doubt. Well, I do face doubts from time to time, though they never really threaten to do me in. I face them openly, whenever they come around, for the sake of deeper certainty. And now that my good fortune and yours are connected by the threads of fate that run through all of humanity, I want to encourage you to ask yourself: "What will I do if I don't win the lottery?" And when you find the answer, write it down and follow it faithfully – all the way to the riches you deserve.

The Elixir of Extended Life

✳   ✳   ✳

Ink to paper… cobalt blue, or call it midnight. Either way it is the elixir of extended life – and more, so much more – a roadmap to the soul whenever we speak our truth in solitude. On cloudy days I spill sunlight onto empty pages and watch thought waves become heat waves in the midst of a winter storm. I've known turbulence, tedium, and torment, as well as the warm and vital energy of serenity. I've wrestled with grand abstractions, on land and at sea.

But I could not for the life of me find my way in the Midwest. I didn't belong there. So I left, although I do so honor the many memories I carried with me when I moved west and found the life that I was meant to live.

California is my home – in the deepest, truest sense of what we imagine, hope, and wish our homes to be. It takes time to fully surrender to the truth of what we wish for, pray for, and aspire to become. It takes time to fully honor our own fates. It isn't easy. It never is – nor is it meant to be. That being said, if it isn't joyful and rewarding for you a significant part of the time, chances are that you have yet to realize the dream that holds the key you need to unlock the door that opens out to the road that leads you through your destiny. And chances are, if the dream that seems beyond your reach keeps moving toward the horizon you keep moving away from, you'll never meet – like the fantasy lover you know you'll never embrace. Its funny how running away from what we think we want tends to keep us from ever really having it. We'd rather call it a mystery and leave it at that. We keep slipping away from what we truly want and accuse *it* of being elusive.

Ink to paper… cobalt blue, or call it midnight. Either way it remains the elixir of extended life – the tabula rasa of true intention I continue coming back to. I've been to sea, and have seen the beauty and the power of more than one ocean. I've watched sunlight dance like golden angels upon a moving cerulean dance floor. I've stood on the upper deck of a good-sized ship, permitting ferocious waves to thoroughly soak me while I pretended to be Ulysses. I've been to sea, but do not call me Ishmael. That name would never suit me, not to mention the fact that Melville claimed it long ago, and it has lasted. My name sounds nothing at all like Odysseus – which is not to suggest that my life has lacked adventure, or that I see it as anything less than my odyssey.

Leviathan lives on land and in the sea; it dwells in the waters of our psyches and swims in our deep imaginations, which makes it part of the lexicon we came in with – part of the language written into and onto the soul. And we need it if we wish to live and tell our own true stories. We need it in order to fully honor our uniquely individual destiny. And what could be more honorable than that?

I have neither the need nor the desire to borrow even a single line from "The Rime of the Ancient Mariner," nor any reason whatsoever to aim my crossbow at an albatross. And I, like Dante in the middle of his journey, have found myself within a forest dark, but not because the straightforward pathway had been lost, but rather because of the time I spent attempting to follow a path I knew I wasn't suited for, denying my intuition and opposing my soul. The straightforward path kept leading me astray until I found my way along the circular path. And so, in the spirit of dear old Mr. Thoreau, who wrote in first person while living alone for a time on Walden Pond, I'm saying this: Ink to paper... cobalt blue, or call it midnight. Either way it remains the elixir of a true and better life.

The Gift of Fate and Surprises that Align Us

✳ ✳ ✳

Books are given as gifts throughout much of the world – for birthdays, holidays, anniversaries, and the occasional just because. Those of us who love to read consider our favored books to be great treasures. When we receive one as a gift, there is a tendency to treasure it that much more. When we choose a book for someone else – a book we wish to give to another – we never really know how powerful an impact it might have on them or how long its scope of influence might last.

I wasn't much of a reader until I turned fifteen. There were a few books I enjoyed reading before that time, but none that moved me enough to help construct and shape the character that would allow me true alignment with my fate. Up until that time, I preferred running, playing, and finding trouble on the streets of old Chicago. I had no deep, undeniable sense of who I was, which isn't unusual at all while we're in the throes of adolescence.

I remember the first book I ever read with a completely open heart and mind – a book that carried me to and through a realm that could not be forgotten. How that wonderful little book came to me in the first place is a rather remarkable story in its own right. It was gifted to me at the age of fifteen by a lovely woman one year shy of twice my age at that time, on a cold, snowy morning in Chicago. It all began with a glorious feast the night before – food and drink and celebration at one of the finest Greek restaurants ever to exist in the metropolitan Midwest: Diana's – a famous, festive, Mediterranean-style restaurant on the southwest side of Chicago.

I was invited to join my sister, her boyfriend, and a friend of theirs I hadn't met before. We arrived at the restaurant and got in line behind thirty or forty people, which was typical and could always be expected at Diana's, where the celebration started right there where you stood. Waiting in line at Diana's was unlike waiting at nearly any other restaurant. Everyone talked, everyone smiled, everyone periodically shouted Opaa! and everyone drank either white or rosé Roditis – provided you were over the age of thirteen. No matter how hungry you felt when you stepped into line, the atmosphere of that well-loved restaurant seemed to pacify even the most starved and impatient patrons. After all, it was really the warm, spectacular ambiance we hungered for most. You could taste the metaphors floating through the air, covered with the delightful scents of fresh-cooked food. How many hours of our lives do we spend waiting without any sense of celebration whatsoever? There are things we have to wait for in this world; it makes sense for us to rejoice while we wait and make the most of the time we've been given.

Finally, after rejoicing in line for nearly an hour, we were seated at a round table in the center of the main dining room near the open-hearth fireplace, which was crafted from ancient stones flown in from Athens, we were told, and was an extraordinary blessing on wintery nights in Chicago. It was also the ideal spot from which to watch Petros, the gracious, flirtatious, irrepressible host, perform the dance of life while balancing a full glass of wine atop his head. For the great, robust, triumphant finale, he would drink the wine from the glass he had kept perfectly balanced throughout the dance, then smash the empty glass into the fireplace. "Opaa! Opaa!" we all yelled, as our well-dressed waiter carried our enormous tray of food to our table for four. Octopus, leg of lamb, dolmades (grape leaves stuffed with flavorful rice), fried squid, roasted bell peppers, cucumbers with feta cheese and mint leaves, and probably one or two other dishes I've forgotten. And as if all that was not enough, another waiter brought us a seemingly magical flaming cheese – held high on route from the kitchen to our table – a soaring fire several feet above our heads adding to the ambiance of myth and magic in an atmosphere of passion and romance.

We ate fine food, drank good wine, and felt the warmth of the fire – on the outside as well as on the inside. We talked openly about the things that truly matter – the things we loved, the things we dreamt about, the things we needed. I was the young one at the table, an eager teen with raging hormones and big dreams. We shared our thoughts, and not once during that lively, joyful, spirited evening did I ever imagine I would wind up spending the remainder of that spectacular night with the woman one year shy of twice my age, though that was, in fact, what followed.

She woke me in the morning to let me know she was going out to get us breakfast and to stop at the bookstore across the street to buy a book she wanted me to have. She left me alone to reminisce about the fullness of that amazing night of passionate celebration. A short time later, she returned with warm French toast, pure maple syrup, and a paperback copy of *Siddhartha*, on which she wrote on the inside cover: *Everyone's looking, few people find. I hope that you are one of those who find. Love, Sophia.*

I never saw her again after that day, though what we shared that night and day will be with me forever. The book she chose for me was the perfect gift for a young man in search of himself, allowing me to align myself with the pathless path we must pave for ourselves – a path that I have paved with poetry and dreams as much as anything – poetry and dreams that rise together, come to life, and keep me aligned with my fate.

Genius and the Beauty of Inspiration

✳ ✳ ✳

When our thoughts seem insipid and our memories lack brilliance, luster, and true inspiration, it is best to then be swept away by someone else's genius. It is good to stand in awe of another's bold creation. Michelangelo's magnificent sculptures of Moses and David, or his flawless Madonna – they are enough to lift nearly anyone from their largely self-induced lethargy. Any sentient being is bound to be moved by what a gifted sculptor brings to life through the use of a hammer and chisel. Should you have the great good fortune to stand before those momentous figures carved from ancient marble, you might, if you stand in awe long enough, be privileged to see those sculptures move. You may even hear the heartbeat of the artist if you're able to find and hold your own inner silence long enough.

And should the residues of accumulative stress and collective tedium still cling to your psyche after that, getting lost in a masterful painting might permit you to shake them loose, if you truly wish to. Perhaps one of Michelangelo's lesser-known paintings, such as *La Catena* – a painting which offers us an artful overview of Florence, the town that some have christened The Cradle of the Renaissance. Or Botticelli's rendition of *The Birth of Venus* may enhance your mood. Or *The Garden of Earthly Delights* by Hieronymus Bosch, or his colorful depiction of *The Ship of Fools*. Then again, Henri Rousseau's lush and primitive delineation of *The Dream*, painted in 1910 – the year he died – might remind you to remember one of your own. Of course, your personal preference may lean toward something by Monet, Cezanne, or Van Gogh; Degas, Renoir, or Manet.

Beauty may well be in the eye of the beholder, but only if the eye is connected with the heart and thoroughly aligned with the soul. Anything less could leave us blind and damage our other senses. Dulling our senses leads to boredom; boredom is a catalyst for fatigue; fatigue tends to rob us of the courage to create; and creativity remains, as a potent antidote to the all-too-typical, habitual inertia. The point I wish to make is simply this: Creativity lifts us into a higher realm, expanding our awareness and inspiring us to offer our own gifts.

When our thoughts seem insipid and our once-bright memories have lost their luster, being swept away by someone else's genius may well be the tonic we need. Getting lost in the beauty of nature – or the nature of beauty – has the power to lift us up and shake us from the lethargy of a point of view that lacks imagination.

The Last Attack

✳   ✳   ✳

As a child I was stricken with severe allergies and asthma that kept me from having, holding, tasting, touching, and smelling a vast array of life's true blessings, such as trees, grass, most plants, many types of flowers, and a rich variety of foods. And keeping a pet – especially a dog or a cat – was completely out of the question. All of my childhood doctors were in total agreement about what I should and should not do: I needed to avoid everything I was allergic to, come in every Saturday morning for my weekly allergy shot, and most of all remember to remain sedentary.

"Do not exert yourself," my doctor told me. "No running, climbing, or strenuous exercise, which are likely to trigger a dangerous attack that could, in fact, be fatal."

I did my best to avoid most of the things I was told I was allergic to, and continued taking the shots, which I began to suspect were worthless. But remain sedentary? Not on your life or my own. I repeatedly disregarded that not-so-sage advice which emphasized the importance of maintaining a less than active lifestyle – in other words, a childhood void of exertion.

"Would you like us to give you a note that would excuse you from gym?" was an offer I declined each and every time my doctor or nurse

was inclined to ask. They had no clue – no awareness whatsoever –
that they were asking me to abandon my saving grace. I played hard,
ran everywhere, rode my bike like a demon, swam every summer, and
trained in gymnastics year-round. I became one of the top gymnasts in
my grammar school. I also set the 50-, 60-, and 100-yard dash records.

At the age of eleven, I told my parents that I would no longer be taking the allergy shots each week. After several years of weekly injections,
I was now convinced that they were not only worthless, but a deterrent
to the wellness I aspired to – a subjective decision based on my own
intuition rather than any information I had read or heard or been told
by anyone I knew at that time in my life.

I told my parents that I would cure myself; that I didn't need the
shots and that they were, in fact, not helping. My parents asked me if I
might want to talk to another kind of doctor; they didn't say psychiatrist,
but that's what they meant. And even though they were doubtful, I got
them to agree to a trial period. "We'll see how well you do without them,"
they said.

But I wasn't through. I begged, pleaded, and finally convinced them to
get a dog – a furry little Pekinese that we all grew to love – and I began to
immerse myself in all the things that used to make me sick (or had been
told would make me sick). I cut the grass for neighbors who didn't know I
had been told repeatedly to stay away from lawns. I woke up and smelled
the roses – literally. I climbed trees and savored those heretofore forbidden
fruits, such as strawberries, which doctors said "could possibly be fatal."

I don't remember my first asthma attack, but I vividly remember my
last. I was eleven years old. It was a humid, hot summer day in Chicago, and I was running wild across the savanna – running hard and

fast through the African jungle (in reality, the alleys behind our house). There were many beasts and potential predators I needed to outrun, some of which were real. Sometimes while playing hard and running fast, especially on hot, sticky days, my lungs would start to swell and squeeze off my air supply. That day was no different in that regard. I decided to leave the jungle, albeit reluctantly, and return home to rest.

I came home to an empty house, a true blessing that allowed for undisturbed, quiet focus – the kind of stillness required for the deep awareness wherein I found my cure. As I lay on my parents' bed, mesmerized by the shiny silver bolt in the center of the fan that stood at the foot of the bed, I began to find my center, too. I looked into the mirror of metal in the middle of the vortex – sharp steel blades spinning and whirling like a metallic dervish, creating a quiet, steady hum. I lay still – centered and relaxed enough to listen deeply to the hum inside my chest, and to the chorus, and the percussion. I was calm enough to hear the orchestra inside myself: flutes, horns, and primitive whistles produced by tiny puffs of needed air struggling through a very narrow passageway. I was as calm as I'd ever been in the midst of an asthma attack. This time, for the first time, it didn't feel like an attack, but rather a private concert in my honor that I felt compelled to listen to. I heard primeval chimes and sacred snare drums – the rapid, rhythmic, crackling sounds of swollen lungs that blocked my air supply.

I was so enthralled by the music inside my body that I forgot to be afraid of my inability to breathe. I was aware, but not fearful. I knew that very little air was getting through – less, perhaps, than at any other time I could remember. Then a dazzling realization came to light, accompanied by the chorus in my chest. I remember thinking, "The little bit of air that is getting through is enough to sustain me. The little bit is all I need. The little bit is enough!" And with that thought and the awareness it carried, suddenly my lungs opened fully and completely. That sensation touched every living cell of my body, echoed through all the halls of my psyche, and danced joyfully in the center of my soul.

It took years for me to finally realize that that had been, in fact, my last attack.

Determining the Destiny
We Question

✳ ✳ ✳

I want to share a story with you straightaway – without poetic embellishment or added color, be it natural, artificial, or some combination thereof. I want to say it as plainly as possible, without making it any darker or lighter than it actually was. I wish to offer as candid a depiction as my honest, vivid memory will permit. If I manage that, I trust it will be enough to let you in on the deep and lasting impact I was left with from the day that I am now about to share with you.

I woke up one morning nearly a decade ago, after one of my rare, rather dark nights of the soul, only to discover that it was far from over. In fact, it started to look even darker in broad daylight. As the sun rose higher and the air got hotter, I couldn't find my light or feel my usual warmth. Dark nights of the soul seem heavier and more ominous when they greet you on mornings bathed in balmy luminosity, while you remain utterly impervious to all the splendor flooding forth. The clouds that follow us around on days like that seem saturated with the questions that must be asked – the questions we must ask ourselves.

Fate may be written for us before we can think and breathe freely, but our destiny is largely determined by what we do – what we choose to devote our lives to. One of the clouds that followed me that day – an ominous cloud, immune to sunshine, disguised as a question (or was it a question disguised as a cloud?) – held the defining question that would shape the course of my life and allow me to honor my destiny. It was dark, it was heavy, and it needed to be asked and answered that very day, without refrain, because my very life depended on it, and that cloud above my head would not go away. The more I looked at it, the more I began to believe it carried within it a bolt of lightening capable of killing my true spirit if I were to answer that dangling question incorrectly. And the question was: "Are you really a writer? Are you or can you ever be a writer of consequence, a writer of substance, a genuine writer who can in fact make a difference?" It was the mother of all questions for me at that moment. It was asking me that most significant question: who I truly am.

I was facing the question that held the power to determine whether or not I would honor my fate – the question I needed to take hold of and be willing to dance with in order to determine my true destiny. And how could I dance with a question like that while the music of my heart was still so eerily silent? "Dance anyway," I heard the artist within me say. "Ask anyway, even if you're afraid to get the answer you may not want."

I wanted to join the ranks of the many writers I admired – the wordy immortals who continue to touch the hearts and minds of men and women century after century. Did I have what it takes to become one of them? Did I have the skill, passion, and necessary discipline to dig deeply enough into the soul of my humanity to lay the ink-stained tracks of something lasting? Did I have something to say worthy of the road I was seeing before me? And if it turned out that I didn't, could I bear that?

It was clearly a do-or-die, moment-of-truth situation, and I had little choice but to bear the weight of it, face the question, and answer it – not only honestly, but also correctly.

Is an honest answer always accurate? Or do we determine what is ultimately true for us by doing what we know we need to do? The gospel of one's life is fundamentally established through the actions we align with our deepest thoughts, infused with all the emotion we need to sustain our greatest visions, goals, and dreams.

I wanted to tell this story in straightforward, no-nonsense, to-the-point fashion, though truth be told, cut-to-the-chase storytelling has never really been my forte. I am, however, fully committed to conveying this story faithfully and accurately all the way to the point at which it ends. It's good to have an ending to point at, but what we discover along the way is always the point.

I needed to leave my house that day before the thoughts contained in that dark gray mass of icy emotion could suck me into the vortex of utter uncertainty that seemed to be getting darker and growing larger every second I sat motionless, overwhelmed by the question. I was beginning to believe that the weight and size of it might put cracks in the walls and shatter the windows in my living room.

So where do you go on a dark day of the soul while living in Southern California? I live not far from Malibu and the soft, sandy beaches that line our Pacific shore, though right outside my front door there is a fertile landscape filled with oaks, evergreens, birch, mimosa, and plenty of plum trees. And across the road there are flowing hills with ample footpaths that wind through another kind of wilderness. I am totally surrounded by lush hills, and a short drive through the canyon leads me to the sandy beaches of Malibu – two very rich possibilities – though that day I opted for the city instead.

I wanted to hang out with some of the robust spirits of the wordy ones – with some of the writers who seem immortal by virtue of what they managed to lay down. After all, I wanted to be one of them – one of the prolific writers who live for centuries. I wanted to be one of the prodigious poet-philosophers who continue to dance in the hearts and minds of the many generations still to come; to be known and loved by those who live in this amazing time. I write because I need to write, though somewhere in the front or back or middle of my awareness is the desire to touch, inspire, and lift the hearts and minds of the many.

So I got in my car and drove to the Bodhi Tree Bookstore, a well-known independent establishment in Los Angeles. I was lucky enough to find a safe and legal parking space waiting for me when I got there – a rare find in that bustling part of town. I grabbed my wallet and my keys and made my way to the bookstore, moving as gracefully as one possibly can with the weight of the world resting firmly on his shoulders.

I made my way to those concrete steps that lead to the creaky door embellished with Tibetan bells that had a hopeful ring as I sauntered in, hoping to find refuge in the company of spirits that live among the shelves. I stepped gingerly across the wooden floor that leads from aisle to aisle, author to author, shelf to shelf. I wasn't looking for any particular author, at least not consciously. My eyes were clouded with the question that seemed to be demanding an immediate answer, and I still couldn't find one on the dark wooden floor my eyes were fixed upon.

Then I looked up... and the one book boldly reaching forward, leaning two or three inches beyond the edge of the shelf, was *Henry Miller on Writing.* And since it reached out to me, I reached back and plucked it from the shelf. Henry Miller had long been one of the writers I admired. Had he been more in touch with his tender, vulnerable, poetic nature, Henry might have been me. I stood in the aisle between M and N, in front of the shelves where Henry Miller and Anais Nin live together. I stood holding that book for a moment, and then opened it at random to the following passage found on page 19:

> *I had to learn, as Balzac did, that one must write volumes before signing one's own name. I had to learn, as I soon did, that one must give up everything and not do anything else but write, that one must write and write and write, even if everybody in the world advises you against it, even if nobody believes in you. Perhaps one does it just because nobody believes; perhaps the real secret lies in making people believe.*

I read that passage and knew immediately that my old friend Henry had written it just for me – at least it felt that way as I stood there at that moment. In fact, those words surged through my veins like intravenous antivenom, saving me from an otherwise lethal snake bite.

The question had been answered. I am a writer – as long as I remain fully committed to my willingness to write. And from that day forward to this one, I have never doubted myself the way I did that day. I've had my doubts since then, though not to the point of seriously considering throwing in the literary towel.

Return to the Tabula Rasa

✳   ✳   ✳

I come back to the tabula rasa every day – or at least I attempt to – by facing the empty page, the wide open sky, and my less cluttered mind when I first wake and sense this undeniable eagerness welling inside.

That may not be a precise definition of the primary, pristine tabula rasa, but it is a beginning; a good place to start; an honest leap into that moment of eternity that awaits us all every day. Blake talked about that – that eternal moment that remains within reach of every sentient being – not every hour of our every day, necessarily, but one perfect instant we manage to separate from the minutia of the seemingly less than miraculous. He didn't say it quite that way, though I doubt Mr. Blake would have any argument with my loose and lively interpretation. Therefore, I'm left to believe that what he meant is intertwined with my own understanding, which sings, dances, and composes poetry within those eternal moments I keep peering and probing into.

Poets and artists tend to find and fully explore those infinite moments more frequently than those who focus on nothing but making money. And those infinite moments we find and tap in to – those are the moments we carry with us throughout our lives and into any possible hereafter. When we come to that bend that looks like the end – those are the instances that give us immortality. Those extraordinary glimpses of eternal grandeur, stored in the body, psyche, and soul, are the keys and the doorways to the timeless dimensions we dream about when we open up and willingly let go!

And so I come back to something akin to the tabula rasa in order to tap in to the eternal moment that awaits us all every day. It may not be a completely blank slate, but I do what I can to clear the debris of yesterday. It may not be what you would call pristine, but there is a purity of spirit and intention that helps me clear the dust of self-denial. There is this desire attached to a vision, a premonition, or a lucid dream that stays with me virtually every step of the way – a rather vivid dream that inspires and wounds me simultaneously. When I know I'm on track, I feel guided a good part of the time by my sense of bliss. And when I'm not, or think I'm not, then agony tends to remind me to take action. Blake said, "He who desires, but acts not, breeds pestilence." That may or may not hold true for you, but having a vision and the desire that keeps it alive is bound to cause us inner turmoil if our action is less than enough to bring it to life.

And so I come back to the tabula rasa in order to give birth to a dream that has been there all along.

Standing upon the Roots of the Miraculous

※　※　※

When the wildflowers just don't seem wild enough, I return to the rub-
ber tree – back to that beneficent buttress tree, with its magnificent
trunk and far-reaching branches – and to those roots that I can stand on.

Sometimes I need those palatial protrusions to remind me to see
the deeply rooted things that rise above. God knows I need that from
time to time. It's all too easy for us to miss what's above while forever
digging deeper into the mystery, which is boundless. There is so much to
notice in every direction that we tend to forget to look. And forgetting
to take notice of the world that surrounds us puts us in collective danger
of shutting down. Sometimes it seems necessary to shut down, or break
down, in order to rebuild ourselves; all robust systems break down from
time to time in order to rebuild themselves.

Being overwhelmed always remains an option, though rarely, if ever,
a wise one. In the meantime we keep digging into the mystery, which is
limitless, while looking for the answers we imagine might be looking for
us. Sometimes we dig past the roots that want to tell us what we need to
know; we go beyond the obvious in search of the miraculous, and miss
the point in the process. That is why I come back to this regal tree with

its lavish branches and noble roots; back to those palatial protrusions well above ground – sturdy roots for me to stand upon and remember to take notice of the world that waits above.

I am not referring to the heavens, the other planets, or the stars that map the fiery trajectory of my destiny. Nor am I disregarding the undeniable influence those radioactive entities have had from the very beginning. I am simply saying, once again, that the tree of life is *any* tree we take the time to truly notice. I cannot imagine a single tree living anywhere on earth that isn't fundamentally rooted to the miraculous.

Today I went back to the buttress tree – back to those amazing roots, those lively protrusions – because I happen to live in close proximity to that astonishing tree of life. I believe that any tree you can touch is the true tree of life – oak, cypress, evergreen, birch, cherry, apple, or peach, or my mimosa, or any of the other deep-rooted sentinels I haven't mentioned by name. They have their own unique colors and characteristics, though they are all beneficent in their own way. They all keep giving indiscriminately, much the way too many of us have been taught to take. They keep giving and we keep taking, though some of us remember to give back. Therein lies the balance of our world. Balance clearly requires giving back.

I return to those roots for the sake of balance, with the desire to give back. Those hearty roots are part of my awareness, and thus part of my world. They are real, they are touchable, and they are sacred. They remind me to take notice of "what is." It's all too easy for us to miss the magnificent and miraculous while digging too fast and forgetting to notice. I feel compelled to make these deep connections every day in order to fully honor what is real. And trees remain one way in which to do it. They are the lively catalysts of true connection with the real forces of life.

When we make those deep, true, sacred associations, we honor our natures and come to deeper understandings of ourselves. And when we do that, we tend to feel connected to essentially everything, because in reality, we are!

Scent, Snow and the Question of Destiny

※   ※   ※

I feel the need to pluck another primary memory from the archives of my personal history. It's a rather old one – not as old as Mnemosyne, but old enough – a memory born long before I learned to turn the abstracts upside down for the sake of making sense of what I see – an extended moment etched in time during the tender, early hours of my life – an experience that has been inextricably woven into the many timeless fibers of my awareness, for reasons that will be understood once the story you're about to step into has been faithfully unfolded by the only storyteller capable of telling it.

It was the winter of the third year of my life. I'm not entirely certain what month it was, though the snow on the ground and the chill in the air makes me want to guess that it was January. January tends to be a cold and snowy time of year throughout much of the Midwest, which is where I began the odyssey of this life. I was born in the Windy City – Chicago, Illinois – great museums, fabulous food, a famous lakefront, and two of the tallest buildings in the world, neither of which had yet been built at the time this story takes place – a story which may seem small next to a giant skyscraper, but remains meaningful, if not monumental, in my memory.

On that snowy day in old Chicago, I visited a bakery with my mother. I remember being carried part of the way, leaning my hood-covered head against her woolen-coat-padded shoulder, moving through that winter world, smiling at the cold that could not touch me. It didn't stand a chance against my coat, hood, mittens, and the warmth of my mother. There's something magical about staying warm in the middle of winter, feeling impervious to those icy winds that wield the power to make us shiver if and when we are not dressed appropriately or lack proper love and affection – although the latter produces a deeper and more agonizing chill, without a doubt.

I walked into the bakery on my own ahead of my mother, mesmerized by the scent of freshly baked cookies, cakes, breads, and pastries wafting through crisp winter air. My mother grabbed a number, got me a cookie, and we took our place in line and waited for our number to be shouted.

It was my fourteenth season outside the womb, a time when strangers were not instantaneously suspect, especially elders like the crone my mother spoke to while we waited – the old women she asked to keep an eye on me while she placed her bakery order. The haggard old woman wearing heavy, dark clothing was all too willing to oblige. "Come stand over here," she said, "away from the glass, so people can see what they want." I knew what I didn't want, which was to be standing near the rear wall of a busy bakery with a three-hundred-year-old woman dressed in black. I'm sure she wasn't really as old as all that, but she seemed ancient to me at the time.

"What's your name?" she asked – a simple question that I was fully prepared to answer. "My name is Wayne," I told her. "Wany?" she replied in a questioning tone. "No. My name is Wayne," I told her once again. And from that simple, standard question, which I had now answered twice, came the second question – a monumental leap to one of the deepest and most perplexing questions we can ask a child of any age: "What do you want to be when you grow up?"

The instant I heard her ask the question, I knew the answer, regardless of my age, innocence, and presumed naivety. I knew at that very moment what I wanted to be, and I didn't hesitate to proudly tell my not-so-grand inquisitor. I stood straight and tall in my three-foot frame, looked directly into the old woman's watery eyes, and told her, "I want to be a lion!" "A lion," she said, with a look of disapproval and surprise. "You can't be a lion... a lion is an animal. You're a person – a human being. And a human being can't ever be an animal. Do you understand?" I nodded my head yes, hoping to quiet her down and take a moment to feel my disappointment. It wasn't as if I had worked and planned to become a successful lion my entire life – all three and a half years of it. I simply imagined how amazing it would be to be a lion, and I wasn't entirely certain it was not possible, although the crone of a woman who had asked the question made it clear to me that being a lion was out of the question – not an option, hope, prayer, or possibility.

I could still see my mother standing at the bakery counter, taking what seemed like an eternity to place her order. "So, Wany," she still couldn't say my name correctly, "what do you want to be when you grow up?" She was relentless. She wasn't about to give up the question until I got it right.

So there I was, standing near the rear wall of a very busy bakery, held captive by a relentless old woman armed with a question to which she was determined to get an answer. "Wany – Wayne, Wayne... what do you want to be when you grow up?" Now that I had learned and understood the limitations – the laws and physics forever in place, narrowing the options in order to keep us aligned with only the genuine possibilities in regard to what we wish and want to be – now that I knew I could watch lions on television and at the zoo but could not become one, no matter how much I admired them, this time I felt pretty confident that I would answer the question correctly – from my inquisitor's point of view. I stood straight, gathered my thoughts, looked once again into the eyes of my interrogator, and told her, "I want to be an Indian!" Next to being a lion, which I now knew that I could not, being an Indian seemed to be the next best possible thing. Indian men got to hunt with bows and arrows, ride horses without their shirts on, roam free, sleep in tipis, and dance around blazing fires with all their friends. That, to me, seemed like a great way to live – lots of fun, excitement, and adventure.

I felt pretty happy about my second choice. My inquisitor, on the other hand, did not look happy at all. She gave me the unmistakable look of disappointment, disapproval, and disbelief all rolled into one. "You can't be an Indian," she said, with a bit of a sneer. "Why can't I be an Indian?" I asked. "Indians aren't animals. An Indian is a person, like you told me I needed to be." "Because they're not the same kind of people we are," she said. "An Indian is a different kind of person than you. You're white. Indians aren't white... they're red! Do you understand?" No, I didn't – and not because I was only three years old, but because I knew better. I didn't want to understand that rigid distinction between human beings – the primary pigmentary explanation that separates us from our humanity. I didn't share my inquisitor's point of view, and I had no wish to. I was three years old, and I knew better. My life experience was limited, and I was still free of formal education and the typically biased filters that tend to come with it. I was still thinking with the instinct that we are taught to abandon and encouraged to forget for the sake of maturity. Of course, conformity gets mistaken for maturity much of the time.

So... what did I want to do, and thus become, when I grew up? The question of questions, which carries within it the seed of divine potentiality – the energy that moves us from thought to thought, and through the actions required to shape the character needed to define the fate that steers us to and through the destiny we undoubtedly co-create. What do you want to "be" when you grow up? is such an immensely complex question for essentially everyone that many choose a path that may not suit or serve them simply to lessen the weight of the question they feel ill-equipped to answer.

I was five years old the first time I heard Elvis sing. I knew right then and there that I wanted to be a singer. When I turned six, I felt strongly about becoming a doctor. And at the age of seven, I realized that I needed to be a savior. Not *the* savior or the messiah – please let me make that perfectly clear. What I realized at that early age was a need to be the steward of my dreams and the savior of the words that were part of the lexicon I came in with – the language written into my soul. I felt compelled to tell a true and meaningful story that I had yet to fully live – an inspirational, true life story – and claim it as my own.

Of course, a real life story can't be claimed until it has been lived sufficiently, and that takes time. It takes courage and necessary struggle. It requires a unique form of faithful openness to live the many moments of our lives as fully as possible – the mundane and the miraculous, the ordinary and the exalted, the painful instances we wish to pass through quickly, and those pivotal moments of bliss we attempt to prolong. We need to live them all as completely as possible in order to sustain the memories we must return to in order to tell our stories truthfully. If that is the fundamental task that you've been given – the primary undertaking that determines the destiny held in your hands – then you must be the messiah of your own unique understanding in order to tell your story faithfully.

It takes courage to live within the openness of your own life in order to become the flow of all your thoughts – the great cascade of true emotion and the sacred amalgamation of all your actions. What we choose to do with the life we've been given – that, more than anything, becomes our story. And if we think and think, but fail to act, our lives become stories of collective regret. A full life, a real life, a true life, involves a magical mix of ups and downs and twists and turns that lead us through multiple moments of supposed failure and into our hours of success.

Its seems like an eternity since I stood in that busy bakery waiting for my mother, attempting to figure out what I wanted to be when I grew up. I have lived through many amazing transformations since that day that have lead me to this one; from my desire to be a lion, an Indian, a singer, and a doctor, finally to my desire to be the savior of my own thoughts and dreams. That, of course, is the short list, as opposed to the long list of real life options and possibilities I considered along the way. There was no way to know the lasting impact of that anything-but-mundane stop along the way at three years of age. There was no way to know how long I'd be haunted by the question I was asked that day. There was no way to know that all of my collective thoughts and actions that followed after would make me into the writer I've become – the impassioned poet and brother to the baker, by virtue of the essential task of nourishing the many hungry souls who share my world, this world, our world.

Recognition

※　　※　　※

I recognize this precipice –
stunning as an ancient
memory that cannot be forgotten.

I'm rather familiar with
this precipitous stance –

this romantic preparation
for another inevitable leap.

I know this cliff-top, and
the intrepid dance that is
done along life's precious edges.

I know this view – this artful
perspective, creative landscape –
airbrushed by a willful glance.

I've been here more than a
million times, and
it's the first time every time.

Fate, Recollection, and Solitude

❋ ❋ ❋

Sometimes I feel too much like the lone pine standing at the summit of a lesser-known mountaintop, having burst into the world through a womb of solid rock. I've been up there. I saw it touching the clouds with its evergreen fingertips, leaning east or west depending on the direction of the wind. And as beautiful as the world appears from five thousand feet above sea level, I wouldn't want to stand there alone for two or three hundred years.

Fortunately I am a man with moveable roots. I sprang from a fleshy womb as opposed to an earthy womb of dirt and solid granite. Still and all, I've stood alone on numerous occasions, and I've walked alone more times than I can remember, and danced alone from time to time while singing or humming to myself. And of course, I sit alone for hours every day for the sake of saying something that I haven't said before. I've climbed trees, mountains, and modern brick buildings alone; sat atop ladders, walls, and rooftops alone; hiked alone, ran alone, swam alone; explored caves alone, on land as well as a few beneath the sea; and I've laughed alone at least as often as I've cried. Once, and only once, I was daring or insane enough to hang alone by a single hand from the jutting branch of a regal tree, staring down at a two thousand foot drop to ancient layers of multicolored rock. There's something extraordinarily enlivening about holding your life and death in a single hand, trusting the strength, power, and certainty of your own grip.

You may be wondering if I felt the least bit tempted to let go while hanging freely above the great Grand Canyon by a single hand, holding on to a seemingly sturdy branch of a regal tree growing out of the side of its north rim.

Crazy as it may have been, I assure you it was a life wish, not a death wish – a death-defying moment wherein I chose the fullness of life consciously and deliberately, deeply and profoundly moved by the ante-diluvian beauty of such an astonishing view. I could feel real life flooding through me, and I loved it! And that's what I've been choosing ever since, every day, throughout the decades that have followed.

Now I sit alone at my writing table telling stories to myself while piecing together the memorable moments that lend vibrant color to the fullness of my irrepressible awareness. Alone at last… again and again with my effervescent thoughts and recollections; alone with all my lofty dreams and deep desires to do more, to give all that I can while I'm alive. I am alone with my back pain and periodic heartache; alone with my fertile collection of fallen pine cones that I lifted from the ground after a wind storm; alone with the lexicon I was born to give birth to within this life that I've been given; alone with my coherent accumulation of serendipitous instances, and with my significant stockpile of synchronistic occurrences that stay fresh and vital in the archives of my aliveness. I am alone with my sensations of primal solitude – the all-inclusive, ever-unfolding mysterium continuum. I am alone once again with my many muses – dancing, writhing, and smiling for me, encouraging deep, authentic, artful expressions from the heart and soul of the poet I was clearly meant to be. I am alone with my hilltop view of budding trees surrounded by wildflowers, and halcyon swans floating freely across the murky surface of the lake in my backyard, while horses graze and koi swim slowly beneath the threshold of our collective consciousness. I am alone with my pure, profound, and prolific awareness of the goddess who waits for me and me alone. So how alone could I possibly be with all of this? Only as alone as fate requires me to be – as alone as I am willing to be to fulfill my true destiny.

Gypsy Dreams and Bohemian Memories

* * *

Maybe my mother really did want to live among the gypsies, if only for a little while – like a kind of vacation on one of the lesser-known islands of the world. Maybe she just needed a hiatus from the routine that consumed her – a brief or extended pause from the monotony of attempting to live an acceptable life. Maybe she secretly wished to live among and be one of the vagabonds – one of the wanderers who never fully settle down.

That would explain why she saw gypsies nearly everywhere she went. They followed her from Ohio to Illinois; from her Cincinnati home town to the famous Windy City of Chicago. Wherever she went, the gypsies only she could see were sure to follow. Maybe she really wanted a rich, nomadic life – the freedom to move from place to place without ever settling into a fixed routine in a fanatically well-kept, stiflingly permanent residence. Maybe her true heart held the courageous spirit of the wanderer – the adventurer with a passion for the new. And maybe those gypsies continued to follow her around to remind her of who she truly was – an Irish-Italian singing Bohemian from the metropolitan Midwest.

But her Bohemian spirit, which longed for discovery, settled for something quite different from the dream that prompted her to leave home in the first place. That seems to be what most of us do; we dream, move toward it, and then shrink back when the reality comes too close. We fantasize about the bold adventures we think we'd like to have, traveling first class within the comfort and safety of our lofty imaginations. Most people manage to get that far, though fail to follow through on the half-made plans they less than wholeheartedly make, and wind up settling for something less than to their liking. We call it compromise, and defend it simply by saying it was necessary. Sometimes it is. Sometimes we settle some of the chaos of our lives through our willingness to make a few concessions. There is an obvious need for honest compromise with a sense of fairness that permits us to have and hold the true or false perception of a win-win situation. Compromise can be an honest response to the pressures of life, allowing us to do and have certain things – always at the expense of others. Though far too often, from my perspective, compromise is used as a flimsy excuse for a lack of commitment to follow through wholeheartedly on a dream or goal or lofty vision that could, in fact, be viable.

I could go deeper into the psychology of our collective excuses for settling into lives that don't please us. But I need to get back to those gypsies who unremittingly shadowed my mother throughout her life. I have to wonder – and can't help but imagine – that part of her really did want to live among them, or merely more like them. She was a Catholic girl by indoctrination, who fled Cincinnati in the middle of the night to pursue the dream she thought might be found in the Windy City. And what is that if not an act of courage, prompted by the adventurous spirit of the gypsy who lived within her? And so a young, beautiful, singing Bohemian, who some years later became my mother, was well on her way toward the dream of a better life… good for you, Mamma! Good for you. How could I do anything other than smile and applaud your act of courage.

So my mom-to-be made it to the Windy City. Now what? Where might she locate a life that looked more like the dream she left Cincinnati to pursue? She wanted to be a singer. That was her passion – an Italian, Irish, Catholic girl from Ohio who had studied both opera and jazz. With youth on her side, the gift of song, and a bright dream dancing in the center of her psyche, she found the courage to make the leap that landed her in Chicago. Of course, even young, aspiring singers need to eat, and Chicago was filled with fabulous restaurants, forever in need of pretty waitresses filled with hopes and dreams. So she served food to customers, with a hopeful smile and a song in her heart that became fully audible from time to time when she was no longer able to contain it. She smiled, sang, and served food to customers in a downtown restaurant while praying she'd be discovered by a big-time talent agent and bid farewell to waitressing.

In the meantime, those eager gypsies were still waiting in the wings, nodding their heads and waving her toward them, beckoning her to join them while she still could. She must have considered it a number of times, even though the gypsies probably frightened and excited her simultaneously. Who wouldn't be tempted, albeit secretly, by the kind of freedom they represented – the kind of autonomy we love to talk about but tend to abandon rather early in life. We trade in that freedom and autonomy for a sense of security that typically turns out to be false. Like the ageless poets and sages say: "A false sense of security is the only kind there is."

Dreams often lead to realities we never imagined – until the day they surround us on all sides. And there we are – right in the middle of a life we didn't envision or fully prepare for. I suppose the best way to prepare for an unplanned life is to expect the unexpected and do our best to embrace it when it arrives. Heraclitus said, "Expect the unexpected, or you won't find it." I wholeheartedly agree with the first half, but I have to question the second. (I respect and appreciate those ancient philosophers far too much not to think beyond the wise and beautiful quotes we wish to remember.) So expect the unexpected – yes! But I think we're bound to find it whether we've learned to expect it or not. To expect it is to be better prepared to honor it when we do.

I'm sure that my mother never expected to meet a crazy, charismatic, tough Russian Jew from Chicago – via somewhere in the harsh U.S.S.R. – but she did. When she dreamt about a singing career while feeling trapped in Cincinnati, I'm rather certain she didn't envision the wild man with a fondness for gambling, a love of animals, and little or no patience for human beings – the man she fell in love with and wound up marrying. Less than two years later she gave birth to a blue-eyed baby girl. Then three years later, on Fathers' Day, I came into the world with an array of dreams I've come to realize as my own.

Many of my richest dreams have been realized and are being lived and fully cherished by the awakened dreamer as we speak. I dreamt of having a family of my own. And I couldn't dream of a better wife and true best friend than the girl I met in high school and later married. And never in a million years and a thousand lifetimes could I have dreamt of having two sons as magnificent as the ones I have been blessed with. I dreamt about being a writer, an author, and an impassioned public speaker – dreams that became the reality that continues to guide my life and fill in all the timeless hours of co-creation with an unequivocal sense of meaning.

And so my mother saw, or thought she saw, gypsies nearly everywhere she went, never fully realizing she was one of them – in spirit, if nothing else. And what else is there?

Adding My Thoughts to a Conspicuous Canvas

✳ ✳ ✳

Clouds are busy painting mindscapes onto a pale blue ethereal canvas. Pine trees are wearing morning dew – a translucent coat to attract the sunlight finding its way through those winter clouds. The dark decanter stands ready to pour bright possibilities over the fertile landscape of the creatively open mind. Black oaks stretch upward and outward through morning fog – deep-rooted sentinels offering shelter to wood nymphs; tall, sturdy, reliable landmarks for poets, sprites, and lovers to dance around.

If you keep moving west, you'll come to a half-frozen waterfall flowing into an intermittently icy creek. Come spring, those waters which seem not to be moving will melt, and much of what appeared stagnant will be bound to run wild in its own time. Once our fears begins to thaw, we feel free. And when we feel free enough, we find love. When we're truly free, we are love. With that awareness comes a bigger and better list of responsibilities along with a lavish catalogue of heretofore unfathomable wonders – wonders that never cease to astonish those who continue to pay attention to all the marvels of the mystery that surrounds us.

Don't be duped by the legendary inventor who told us, "Success is

10 percent inspiration and 90 percent perspiration." It's been taken out of context and used repeatedly by greedy, self-serving, shallow men and women in middle and upper management – those who feel driven by the desire to dominate and control all the hard-working wage slaves they have the audacity to look down upon. We ought to be inspired to perspire – the way that Edison was. We are better prepared to invent, create, and contribute to humanity when we feel strongly connected to our sense and source of inspiration. When we're inspired to perspire every step of the way, we might then look back and be able to say, as Thomas Edison did, "I never did a day's work in my life. It was all fun."

A cornucopia of great good fortune is often the result of a chance opportunity coming in contact with adequate planning and preparation along with a fundamental vision that continues to keep us alive! Now I'm on my balcony, peering into the infinite, looking into this bright, ethereal, cloud-painted canvas, falling through time-eternal and into this beautiful mystery – this magnificent vision that is flooding a precious moment of inexplicable luminosity that I feel privileged to be part of.

Stale Bread and Chemical Wine

※　※　※

Does all this talk of consciousness make any real difference at all? It's hard to say; it's hard to know – especially when you think you know that it doesn't. I see all the usual suspects cashing in on the consciousness industry, which they prefer to regard as a movement. Fair enough. I shall heretofore refer to it as the consciousness movement industry, since I am able to recognize both. In the consciousness movement industry I see old ideas dressed in modern clothing – synthetic robes made to mimic silk, worn mockingly over cotton suits or designer jeans and T-shirts that cling tightly to fleshy parrots pretending to speak The Secret language of new thought.

There is a time for everything, I suppose, though these days, if I listen for more than a minute or two to any of the all-too-many new-age-profiting prophets of the day, I tend to want to throw up at their feet. There was a time when I could bear to listen to the empty, recycled, insipid rhetoric repeatedly presented as the latest and greatest mind-blowing gospel, guaranteed to lift the faithful listener into a realm of higher awareness – once they learn to think for themselves precisely the way they've been told to!

Who isn't sick of all the stale bread stuffed into clean new bags with faintly legible expiration dates that represent the bag, but not the bread? The bread is stale, regardless of the bag it's put into. Seeds, on the other hand, remain fertile for thousands of years, retaining their potency century after century, though once they've been sprouted, cut, and turned into grain that is made into flour used for baking our daily bread... at that stage it's only really fresh for an hour, or maybe a day. Savor it! I do, every day.

I refuse to eat stale bread, even when I'm really hungry. When we're truly hungry we need nutrients, as opposed to filler. We could eat cardboard made to look like hearty, wholesome, ten-grain bread, but it wouldn't taste like fresh-baked bread, and it certainly would not sustain us. Eating stale bread is only marginally better in that the body does recognize it as an actual food source, even though most of the one-time nutrients have been rendered inert – like the language that is steadily reiterated by the many pseudo-new-age prophets of the day – the ones who have no qualms about scraping mold from the bread they package and sell as freshly baked.

And that is the bread – the daily bread consumed by the masses – that coats the tongue as well as the mind with a rather unfavorable residue – a residue people attempt to get rid of by rinsing it down with chemically fermented wine. That is what passes as the sacrament these days: stale bread and quick wine, chemically fermented to save the time that no one seems to have these days – the bread and wine that suits our modern lifestyle of perpetual hurry-up and worry-while-you-wait.

I'd like to think that it's possible for people to meditate their way out of self-induced madness and the various terrors that tend to come with it. I'd like to think that we have what it takes to will our way out of and away from war, and to wean ourselves from the mindset that keeps causing it. I'd like to think that we'll wake before rendering humanity obsolete. What would Jesus say? What would Rumi do? How would Sophia respond if she were here right now? Wait a minute... she is here! Let me ask her. Let me watch her a while and see if she reveals any definitive information through her movements. And I think I know what Jesus would say... but I won't tell you because I think it would probably be a waste of time for those of us who already know, and cause further outrage and fuel the hatred of those who flat-out refuse to. I wish not to support the pseudo prophets, nor offer any energy to fanatical zealots with a fixation on the end of the world. And as far as knowing what Rumi would do, it's rather obvious. He would be busy writing poetry — different in style, though much the same in spirit, as my own.

Back to the Abstracts

※　※　※

It's easy enough for us to come back to the abstracts while the clouds and fog are still hugging the morning like a mistress – like a lover or long-lost friend. Of course, it makes perfect sense for us to turn them sideways or upside down for the sake of seeing them directly from a different point of view. And if and when the wild abstractions lead you back to innocence, don't be too surprised. If surprise does find you, let it wash over you like a new wave. Let it caress you like a loving father or mother who lives to nurture. Let it brush over you, soothing your skin like a lasting breeze after a full day of summer sun. When the windows are wide open and the dusty screens have been aptly removed, the spirit you've been longing for will enter in. And the cup that's been waiting for the guest we can't see will be emptied once again, then naturally filled with the ambrosia of the hour.

It seems as if I've been watching this process for at least a thousand years, wonder colliding with emptiness while clarity dances joyfully through the fog. It seems as if I've been watching this astonishing ritual for no less than a millennium, and after all this time – after what seems like ten lively, colorful, complex centuries – I still rely heavily on pure, euphoric, heartfelt language to touch upon the power of the soul. Language never ceases to move me deeply, in ways I can only convey through the rapture of poetry. I cover the walls of my vibrant psyche with the lexicon I was born to give new life to – fresh energy, fresh breath, fresh order – barrowed from the foundation of sounds and syllables that permeate the soul of the poet and sacred storyteller.

It's easy to come back to the abstracts on a cloudy day, though no less effortless on balmy, cloudless days overflowing with sunshine and shadows, or on partly cloudy afternoons filled with passion and promise, in the robust center of everything – where we go to ask for forgiveness and have the great good fortune to find it. It's the same place we go to offer forgiveness to others who need it as much or more than we do – to the heart that covets nothing that isn't already there.

It's easy to return to the abstracts on a morning like this, while the stony walls of an ancient sea cave are being silvered by pale blue filtered light, while I face the profoundly vibrant beauty of my personalized prophesy being birthed moment to moment by the light of my awareness. Then when those abstracts that I dare to look into lead me back to the heart and soul of innocence, I take a moment to sing and dance and drink a toast to infinite creativity – the eternity of the artist who lives within us all.

Take a moment, which could lead to a lifetime of thoroughly suitable celebration, for the vital effervescence of who you truly are – a free, unfettered, fully connected, boundless spirit of artful resiliency! Then as the world unfolds moment by moment, you can catch the quixotic splendor of this life we've been given and miss next to nothing at all.

The Gift Not Given

✳ ✳ ✳

Sooner or later the precious gift we carry within us must be given fully, because the gift not given becomes a terribly weighty thing, and when repressed, neglected, or denied for too long, it turns into something else – something much less to our liking most of the time – an awful morphing of our deepest creative longing.

The gift not given fully and freely creates an undeniable sense of agony, and then gives rise to our awareness of ecstasy the instant we find a way to deliver it to those we intuitively know it's meant for. Passion, unexpressed, becomes the opposite of ecstasy, the other side of euphoria, the metaphorical wall around the courtyard of our bliss. The gift not given keeps us outside that courtyard, staring at a seemingly solid and impenetrable wall, wondering how in the world we will ever get beyond it. Where's the door, for heaven's sake? Where's a ladder when you really need one? And what did I do with the climbing rope I often carried with me throughout my adventurous adolescence? What became of those glorious wings designed by old daddy Daedelus – the ones that he and his beloved son both used to get beyond the labyrinth they were imprisoned in? I do recall what became of the wings used by Icarus. He flew too high and forgot his father's warning, allowing caution and reason to be over-ruled by the excitement of flying high, too near the sun, which caused the wax that held those wings together to melt, followed by that fateful fatal plunge into the Aegean. But what became of the wings his father used? Maybe Daedelus would allow me to borrow them just this once. After all, I'm a father too, and an inventor in my own right, though with scant mechanical skill.

If I had wings right now, I'd fly above and beyond this wall and land safely in the center of my bliss again – the ecstasy of landing exactly where I belong! Then again, if truth be told, I'd have to confess that this wall was my invention, my construction, and my design. I know its weak spots better than anyone else. There are sections I could walk straight through if I decided to. So what am I waiting for? That's the real ques-tion. After all, I designed this wall that wraps around the courtyard wait-ing beyond it – the sacred habitat that contains the conditions and all the necessary elements to create the bliss that I must claim for myself. I think it impolite to keep it waiting any longer. I built this wall to help protect the things that truly matter most, not to keep me from them.

We need to be awake and aware, and to take the necessary precau-tions while moving the treasures we carry within us through the world. One should never be careless with one's gifts, nor protect them to the point of rendering them lifeless and obsolete by keeping them unavail-able for too long. Creative expression is an ongoing challenge, and mak-ing what we manage to bring forth widely available to those with whom we feel the inherent need to share it tends to be the greater challenge for me, as well as for nearly all the other artists I know.

The gift not given fully and freely becomes a painfully weighty thing, part of the privileged burden of our artful obligation. The gift that holds the power to free us also holds the power and authority to imprison us when we refuse to follow the law of giving freely. Today I intend to ascend these walls around my bliss and claim what waits beyond them. I'll find a way over or under my own construction, or walk straight through it if I really decide to. I've stood outside the courtyard of my bliss long enough, put off by these flimsy walls of limited imagination. I could turn all the bricks to dust if I chose to, and I have! Now watch the wall upon the big screen of the mind turn into a dust cloud on a less compelling horizon. Now go kiss and hug the bliss that you've been waiting for.

Movement, Emotion, and the Music of Life

✳ ✳ ✳

It's easy enough to find angst in our world; no need to send out a search party to locate the roots of our discomfort or discover the whereabouts of our perpetual apprehension. Confusion tends to travel with angst an awful lot of the time, so chances are that you'll find them both hanging out around the places you feel compelled and afraid to go. And I think you know exactly what I mean, not that knowing is likely to stop you from pretending, imagining, and attempting to convince the less authentic part of yourself that you absolutely need a renowned cartographer to map the thoughts and emotions you've yet to claim as your own.

Those feelings, notions, and ambient inklings are reliable coordinates, let's not forget – no less so than the imaginary lines of latitude and longitude, or a magnetized needle pointing north. Of course, they do change and shift from moment to moment, those fleeting sensations that carry awareness, like the notes Vivaldi borrowed and arranged for *The Four Seasons*.

We are symphonies – each and every one of us in our own way – 6.5 billion symphonies playing simultaneously in the middle of all this! Or maybe we're merely the fleshy vessels of great potential, carrying these exquisite chords of comprehension in the hallowed hollows of our hearts, the ardor of pure awareness being steadily pumped through every vein and vital organ of our beings.

Some say music lives in the blood. I have scant inclination to argue otherwise, but I would also say that it lives in the bones and sinews, as well as in the psyche and soul. We feel it on our skin when we really listen. But it goes deeper than that, and we know it. Music carries the sounds of human emotion; it lifts us up, takes us somewhere, and sometimes moves us to tears. Emotion has *motion* in it, and that's the point. We are not single notes, nor are we meant to be. We are symphonies. Or at the very least we hold the potential to become symphonic.

Music is a moving thing that represents aliveness – the journey we call destiny and the power we call fate. Stagnation, on the other hand, is quite the opposite; it is the silent, bitter enemy of fate. Fate cannot be fully realized without our willful participation. People live and die every day without ever really knowing their true destinies. Destiny is what we choose to do with the fate that we've been given. Destiny and free will are inseparable. What we think and feel and act upon breathes new life into the premonition that gave rise to the journey that shapes and determines the outcome of a life.

It doesn't matter if we start with angst and follow our confusion along an uncharted path. The point is that in doing so, we keep moving. And movement isn't merely the sacred force that sparks momentum, but the essential definition of life itself.

Creation as Opposed to Restoration

✳ ✳ ✳

Art for the sake of art can lead us to a practical insurgency – if we're lucky. I think our world is in dire need of a really good rebellion. I believe we are long overdue for a truly inspiring uprising – a magnanimous mutiny that every honest, even semi-conscious citizen senses is sorely missing.

Of course, many imagine that it's merely their excess stress and lack of sleep that's causing them to want to revolt against whomever they see as their oppressors. And thus the battle rages on inside their minds while they bite their tongues and quietly acquiesce.

It's easier to get upset with the one you accept and see as your boss than to face one's own repression. But either way, the urge for something better remains prevalent. The problem is that most people believe and remain thoroughly convinced that money makes it all better. So they suppress the lively spirit that wants to rebel, and work longer and harder for the raise they hope to get. If they keep it up without complaining too much or being overtly attached to their own identities, they may be offered promotions that allow them the illusion of greater freedom, which is not an uncommon phenomenon in the warped, though often wondrous work-a-day world.

Now let's get back to the kind of revolution I believe we truly need. To begin with, I think we all need to pay close attention to our own sense of astonishment. If you don't know what that is, you need to find out so you can follow it. Chances are, if we follow our astonishment faithfully, it will reconnect us with the spirit of who we are. And what in the world could be more important than that? We need to be in awe of our own intuition. We need to be inspired by the breadth of our own understanding. We need to be willing to renounce what rings false within the great halls of our hearts. If we do that, then true revolution will begin. If we do that – and I think we must – the fertile seeds of a practical insurgency will be deeply planted and begin to sprout.

We've seen far too many impetuous revolts prompted by lofty visions fueled with passion and promise that was destined not to manifest at that time – too many hasty uprisings lacking the necessary planning and proper reason required for robust, beneficial change – the kind of transformation we need now.

We are at the threshold of what must be brought about, and we are the ones who need to see it through. We are all participants in the shift toward our survival; consciously or unconsciously, we are part of it. However, acting together in a conscious manner increases our chances for success a hundredfold.

We stand poised for the many changes that must be made; if we don't – if we refuse to participate in the shift toward survival – there's an awfully good chance that we won't. We are the ones who need to decide to do what must be done, because we're running out of options rapidly.

We need an antidote to the sickness of willful destruction – behavior modification on a rather grand scale. Peak oil, global warming, and the spoils of war remain inextricably connected. And our nasty habits have made generous contributions to the problems that could lead to our extinction. There are those who fervently believe it's already a done deal – that we've gone too far beyond the Rubicon, from which there is no turning back.

That is not a belief I feel ready to embrace. Nor do I feel the need to. I'm too stubborn to be that fatalistic. I recognize the seriousness of our personal and collective actions; they do make an impact, and I wouldn't argue otherwise. Based on the impact we've made already, I see the situation that our greed got us into, and I know it's not another Y2K. There are genuine threats to our survival, though I don't believe they're insurmountable at this time.

We need to harvest the thoughts, dreams, and imaginings that nourish, enlighten, and lift us into realms of pure awareness. I'm not talking about a second Renaissance, or any kind of artful déjà vu, but rather a steady cascade of fresh ideas – a lively surge of healthy, constructive, coherent concepts in concert with our shared determination to bring them to life. I'm talking about a supreme stream of undeniable, viable possibilities about real transformation, as opposed to simply another forced resurgence that remains incapable of sustaining us.

I'm talking about creation as opposed to restoration, like when a structurally unsound public facility is condemned and demolished so that something new and better can be built; a fresh coat of paint on a crumbling building is senseless, and will never do.

The Day Before Tomorrow

✳ ✳ ✳

Today may well be the
perfect day in which
to honor and bless the

courageous spirit of
artful innocence that
sings what can't be
said, urging somnolent

sons and drowsy daughters
with gypsy souls to move
like silent wind beyond

where they've been and
into the beautiful mystery
of the yet to be known.

This could well be the
ideal instant to delve into
the realm opposite déjà vu –

wherein nothing at all
is the least bit familiar –
permitting us to see the
world as if it's all completely new!

Not So Hot Pursuit

✳ ✳ ✳

There's something about a rain-washed world that makes my own emancipation seem all the more meaningful – all the more universal. Give me liberty or give me the best hallucination one could have, though I suppose an intermittent mix of both is all we can really hope for or expect as we touch our tongue to the cauldron of history in order to stir the life within us.

Fate emerges from the inside out, like the dreams and hopes and visions that we make manifest, and not unlike the plans which seemed like apparitions and continued to elude me year after year until I finally tired of chasing after them, though once I stopped running away from what I thought I was pursuing, it wasn't long before my faithful dreams caught up with me. When we run in frenetic circles in pursuit of our fates, it's difficult to know who's chasing whom. Running in circles in search of ourselves creates a blur that doesn't lend itself to clarity. We need to stop periodically in order to settle into our true centers long enough to see. We see better with a sense of our own equilibrium; from that vantage point we begin to see that circles have no clear and obvious beginnings that can possibly lead us to absolute ends.

Once we permit that awareness to touch the spirit of who we truly are, it becomes a matter of joyful momentum as much as anything else. Then we may find ourselves in a rain-washed world full of wonder, and we may begin to realize that the radiant hereafter isn't beyond our earthly life, but inextricably woven into the miraculous fabric of here and now – every leaf, every raindrop, every breath.

So how do we get there? How do we settle into our true center long enough to see and thus restore our equilibrium? How can we learn to relinquish our dependence on How To books and seminars, and really start living our lives? That's the obvious question few people I know have stopped to ask, and in our day and age I really think we need to. We are intended to be more than incessant tool collectors running in fervent circles in pursuit of the ghosts we've become but cannot catch, or illusive shadows chasing after silhouettes we're afraid to encounter in the flesh while the endless beauty and miracles of everyday life get mixed into the neurotic blur of never-quite-enough. People chasing after all the things they've been taught they're supposed to want is not an uncommon phenomenon.

The pursuit of happiness continues to lead us astray unless we take the time to define it for ourselves. Once we do – once we commit ourselves to our own understanding – then we're able to give up the ghost and free ourselves from the fruitless pursuit of what we may not truly want and never really needed in the first place. The pursuit of happiness is little more than a futile setup for those who haven't taken the necessary time to define it for themselves. Just look up the word *pursue* in any standard dictionary and you're bound to have a better understanding of why, though since I have already, I'll share my findings with you: *pursue*.

1. to follow in order to overtake, capture, kill, or defeat. There it is in black and white on page 950 of my ever-reliable Webster's. (Go look it up for yourself if you don't believe me. In fact, go look it up even if you do; it's good for us to see things for ourselves.) We see people perpetually defeating, capturing, and killing their own happiness, while remaining utterly clueless as to why it is killed. Stop chasing after happiness, and there's a very good chance it will finally catch up with you, allowing you to live the dreams that refuse to let you go.

Insights into the Inner Life of an Openly Guarded Adventurer

True adventures begin and end with what we hold within. I'm not entirely certain where that idea came from or what it might lead me to today, though some uncertainty at this point in time is part of the organic process; in other words – natural. And some degree of uncertainty or sense of the unknown is built in to the robust spirit of real adventure; it's part of the molecular structure of what could be called the DNA of creative exploration.

All we ever really have are those illusory starting points that keep us reaching forever outward from our moment-to-moment awareness. And we move from those starting points through an endless stream of romantic distractions in search of something solid, secure, reliable, and everlasting.

However, searching for stability in an ever-shifting universe tends to set the stage for continual disappointment. After a while we come to realize that the best and wisest thing we can do is learn to recognize and celebrate our disappointments. And in turn, if we do that, we're better prepared and far more likely to honor our disillusionment, which is not merely practical, but also a fundamental step toward enlightened self-discovery. In fact, it couldn't hurt to make available a course that teaches the practicality of honoring our disillusionment; it does no good to honor anyone else's until we first learn to recognize and honor our own.

I think such a course should be part of the standard curriculum of every middle school, high school, and college in existence. Disappointment 101 would be a mandatory class that students would be required to pass before graduating. Imagine the practical and immediate application of a course that could offer a deep understanding of the importance of disappointment without guilt or the all-too-typical tendency to equate disappointment with failure.

It took me over forty years and countless disappointments to tap in to the wisdom that allowed me to recognize, embrace, and finally honor them for what they are: opportunities to learn about life and discover ourselves in the process. If we're willing to learn from our disappointments, we start to see disillusionment as a doorway to the grandeur of true beginning. And true beginning is what we wake to when we're willing to let go of the pain of disappointment and move forward with the spirit of real adventure.

After enough goodbyes to friends and loved ones – a divorce or two, topped with another job loss; after our dog dies and our neighbor's fat, fluffy cat is taken and eaten by bold coyotes; and the oak we thought would stand forever is struck by lightening, then uprooted by a wind storm – little by little we begin to realize that things don't last forever – including us, by the way. When wisdom prevails, we learn to love more deeply and completely than we ever could before. Then we begin to hold the world in the center of our eternally expansive hearts. In that sense we begin again and again, following the lure of fresh distractions into the forest of endless enchantment and through the fog that floats ashore from mystic seas we feel compelled to cross when the spirit of true adventure touches us, and along the few remaining pristine streams that run parallel to dirt-stone paths that wind through roots and shrubs and vibrant wildflowers fertilized by potent stardust sprinkled by those seven daughters collectively known as the Pleiades.

It seems that to some the stardust is nothing more than meaningless twinkling in an endless void of inexplicable nonsense, though for those who know better it is the luminous light within the well-ordered chaos that our skin and blood and bones were formed from – inextricably connected to everything sacredly held within – the very thing that permits this grand adventure to continue.

In Honor of Our Enigmatic Nature

✳   ✳   ✳

I wake, make my leap from bed, then walk back to this table to sit in the center of my world. I sit here in this semi-silence respectfully, with an eagerness that cannot be denied. I sit comfortably in the middle of all these miracles: wind, shadows, dancing plum trees, soft green needles glistening upon the sunbathed branches of undulating evergreens.

And there is so much more that can and can't be said. So much more that can and can't be seen... so much more: ripe fruit dangling from ethereal vines, moved and urged by the tendrils of time that twist and wind around our awareness like the exquisite mystery that it is. Did I mention the light? Did I describe the palette – the array of lively, shifting, indigenous color, splashed and dripped and meticulously painted upon this vast October canvas? Did I mention the invisible hand – the invisible men and invisible women who opted out of the psychotic paradox before mediocrity had a chance to take hold? Did I mention the numerous human options I pay close attention to most of the time? Did I mention the arid ground that my Paleolithic alter ego kneels upon from time to time in my own modern, primordial, ritualistic fashion? And did

I mention how music soothes not only the savage soul, but the tender, robust, sensitive soul who needs it just as much?

Remember the waves you made when you were a child? Remember the ripples steadily spreading outward through your intermittently turbulent adolescence? Remember the sandstorm that surprised you when you over-eagerly stepped into adulthood, leaving you dismayed about the present, confused about the past, and simultaneously excited and fearful about the future you were yet to step into? How do you come to terms with the past you've been denying all these years? How do you reconcile what you want to believe with the bigger truth you're just beginning to recognize?

Do you remember the womb – that perfectly warm aqueous environment you floated in without a care in the world because that was your world? Do you remember any of your mother's dreams or your father's visions? Do you remember what you wanted to be when you grew up? Do you remember where you were the very first time that question of questions was presented to you? Did you know back then? And did you answer? Are you still attempting to figure that one out? Are you awake? Are you alive? Do you feel privileged? Have you ever danced around the tree of life naked, nearly naked, or fully clothed? Have you ever tripped and fallen over a protruding epiphany that stuck to all of your senses like divine glue, encouraging or forcing you to trust yourself and follow your intuition? Do you smile at the face you see in the mirror? Did you ever sing yourself a love song from the ever-awakening center of your soul? Do you revere the mystery you are part of? Have you ever asked yourself for mercy – asked yourself for guidance – without any need or temptation to proclaim yourself an atheist or swear your allegiance to something you can't embrace or truly believe in? Have you ever prayed openly to the beautiful mystery while honoring your enigmatic nature?

Hunting for Monkeys and Furless Metaphors

※　※　※

Searching for words and syntax in the jungles of the mind can seem a lot like hunting for monkeys in the lush and fertile Amazon. Both are wild; both can be cunning; both can climb up into the tip-top branches and make death-defying leaps from tree to tree while I do my best to follow along on the ground, ready to catch them as they free-fall through the canopy, though I am inclined to climb up after them from time to time if and when I feel the need to or when I see no other choice or viable option. They know how to be elusive, out of necessity, just as I do. It's also in their nature to be playful, which is an innate characteristic that greatly enhances their desire and aptitude for survival. It's part of our nature, as well, to be playfully elusive and cheerfully or ruthlessly cunning for the sake of our own skin. It's all about adaptability when we get down to it – how we greet the reality of steady change and embrace it as fully as we can whenever possible.

I hear beating drums on the sandy shores of Xanadu. I want to follow the sound that closely matches the rhythm within me. I want to climb palm trees and gather coconuts. I want to crack open the outer and inner shells and taste the milk of the tropics on a balmy cliff high above the Pacific. We can't return to the lakes of our youth, but we can find shimmering waterfalls along the paths we've never taken before today. Or we may happen upon a pristine pond hidden within a fertile forest that could turn into nothing but fantasy if we fail to see.

There are four full days remaining before reaching the majestic midpoint of the magnanimous month of August – four full days that guarantee radiant change and effervescent breakthroughs for those who keep their promises not to miss them. If we keep our promises to honor them fully, they will lead us to the luminous midpoint with numerous opportunities for us to shine. If we don't, chances are we'll enter into the middle of August less eagerly, less openly, and less inclined to celebrate our glows. …Four full days of nothing but midpoints, if and when we're centered in the moment at hand, at heart, in the only actual instant there ever is.

I intend to honor the treaty I signed years ago – a sacred agreement, a holy covenant between my psyche, my spirit, and my robust ego that longs to conquer far more than it possibly can on its own. I signed a poetic contract with my divided self for the sake of sacred, vibrant, creative unity in the true and steady heart of who I am. And not once have I been tempted to undo, reverse, repeal, or in any way nullify the deal I made wholeheartedly with the passionate, loving, light-filled nature of who and what I am. If I were to find some less than honorable, albeit legal loophole within the lively body of that binding contract I signed eagerly all those years ago, I would fill it in immediately with poetry, and carry on.

And so the search for lively, colorful, truthful language continues, out of necessity as much as anything – the search for sanctified words that act like monkeys who find shelter in the tip-top branches of life-giving trees, like the words that get away from us through our continual misuse. And who could blame them? Why would any lively, robust, consecrated thing want to be made to mean the opposite of what it is truly meant to be? I chase after them because I must! It's in my contract. It's part of the agreement I made to live true to my own understanding, although I would do it with or without a contract, simply out of necessity. I would do it merely for the salary of my salvation – for the simple wages of poetic satisfaction. I have no wish to be a martyr, garrulous or otherwise, or to starve to death for the sake of pure creativity while being cruci-fied upon the tree that offers life. I'd rather climb up into the tip-top branches and leap from there. I'd prefer to free-fall through the fertile canopy, holding on to the words that permit me to fly while tapping in to the incomparable riches of a true and simple life.

Hanging Out with My Lively Dead Friends

✳   ✳   ✳

All my dead friends love to tell me to "keep going, don't give up, get it out there" – Henry Miller, Walt Whitman, and Pablo Neruda, to mention a few. Henry openly tells me, in his inimitable style, that what I think and write and act upon helps keep him alive. And he says that being dead for decades is a relative thing, no less so than the complex relativity of being alive.

Now Walt Whitman is whispering something about reincarnation that's hard to hear over Henry's somewhat cantankerous tone. I ask Walt to repeat it, and he says, "Tell me what you heard." "I think you said that reincarnation is not limited only to those who have died. And that those who claim to be among the living have innumerable opportunities to remake, rebuild, reshape, and reinvent virtually every aspect of their existence." "So you were listening. You did indeed hear every word of what I opted to whisper. Those who count themselves among the living are reborn every day, but fail to notice. And not only the busy ones, but the lazy ones as well. Even the crazy, loveable, creative ones tend to miss more than a few bits and pieces of the grandeur that surrounds them every day. No matter how awake we want to be, we fall asleep repeatedly out of necessity. And falling asleep is part of the rebirth of which I speak."

Most remain lost in their dreams of a better life, floating between the dulcet fumes of an imaginary past and the toxic bouquet of a less than pleasant present, while rarely, if ever, touching upon the innocuous splendor that awaits the adventurous ones. Now I want to say something I feel certain you already know, which is that words have always been, and still remain, an essential part of the internal medicine we are born with. When our internal lexicon lingers too long in our souls, those words and phrases begin to fester like unwashed wounds. They must be written; they must be spoken; they need to be read! Every poetically passionate pen-pusher knows this. We know about the medicine that poisons us if and when we refuse to let it out. We learn, sooner or later, about the lethal effects of steady repression and the torments of perpetual resistance. Hopefully we learn directly from the ecstasy of letting go, like Neruda did through his voluptuous love poems and his song of despair, sung to a cloudless girl in the midst of smoke and endless questions, with silhouettes saying in a balmy tone, "This is what the wind was busy making from all those colorfully illuminated leaves. You are what those breezes created out of stardust, broken branches, and the debris of scattered love."

Pondering the
Nonexistent Entities

What do those nonexistent entities know about faith or love or loyalty? What could they know, frolicking nearly naked across the ancient yellow sands of our psyches? And how did they get there in the first place? Did we conjure them, long ago in a far-away land now lost? Or perhaps *they* painted *us* into existence. Maybe they were searching for something a bit livelier and a lot more colorful than silhouettes or the typically opaque shadows they followed after, but could not catch. Maybe they etched us in warm, wet sand, and then danced around our indented images until the tides rose and washed away the sketches of the day.

Even the most artfully skilled fairies and impassioned wood nymphs can't secure those images etched in sand. Even those that don't exist hold some awareness of that.

So who came first – the fairies, the wood nymphs, or we humans? It must be said, even though most of us know, that there are plenty of fairies who don't believe in human beings. In this day and age, with all our technology and all that we've accomplished, there are still wood nymphs who aren't convinced that we exist or that we ever did. And I believe that every sentient being – including nonexistent entities who think and feel what we won't allow – is entitled to their own opinions, shaped from their own understanding.

Fantasies always seem to precede our various versions of reality. The problem is that many refuse to let go of their fantasies long enough to honor the astonishing realities that are all around them. Even some human beings seem to sense and know the subtle differences between fantasy and reality – a reluctant understanding for many. Admitting it openly… well, that's a different matter. So if fantasies precede our perceptions of reality, I suppose those fantasies could begin with frolicking wood nymphs. Whether they and the fairies that hover above them existed before our imagination gave birth to them is a question not easily answered through logic alone these days. Why rely upon anything as ephemeral as reason, for gods' sake!? Which brings up another well-imagined entity people are expected to believe in. And I mention this not because I proclaim myself an atheist, which I don't – I believe atheism lacks imagination and that orthodox religion has far too much of the wrong kind. I wouldn't argue against the existence of god, divinity, or some supreme being. I simply don't believe in any god that has been manufactured from the tenets of organized religion. Call me crazy, but I'm a bit put off by the notion of an omnipotent being who willfully causes droughts, floods, earthquakes, famine, plague, and pestilence. I find it more than a little problematic that an all-knowing, all-seeing, supremely wise being who is nothing-but-loving has a penchant for sending us disease and great disaster and causing pain, suffering, ultimate anguish, and death to those who praise him daily and those who don't.

So what came first – the chicken, the egg, or the prolific bacterium of intelligent life that turned into human beings? And what do elves have to tell us? What might sprites and imps have to say? What about apparitions and angels – where do they fit in? And when did they come into being? And more important, why? Were they conceived for the sake of living a care-free life, like those nonexistent fairies and half-naked wood nymphs frolicking across the golden-yellow sands of our psyches? Clearly there are far worse fantasies we could conjure than those. When we look around, we can't help but see all the ugly, brutal, murderous fantasies playing out in our world – upon the stage that Shakespeare called "All of life."

Chances are that we created the idea of angels and fairies in order to help us imagine what an ideal life might look like. Wood nymphs may well be an ideal nostrum for an ailing imagination – god knows we need that from time to time. And here we are, back again to that supreme being fantasy that seems almost impossible to get away from – and I feel no particular need to. It's fantasy and imagination no matter what! This isn't to say that I'm unable to recognize, appreciate, and deeply honor my own reality, because I am and I do, though as far as I know, no one has ever been killed because of their notions about fairies or been ostracized for believing in or not believing in angels. Nor has any bloody battle been fought or war been waged over any fantasy regarding wood nymphs.

So the question isn't whether or not god, fairies, and angels exist, but are we willing to live true to ourselves and to our visions of an ideal life? Are we willing to hold true to what we know is possible long enough to see it come to fruition, and then live it with real passion every day? Because without passion it isn't possible to live authentically. The single question that was asked by scholarly Greeks of ancient times about those who passed from this life was: Did they have passion? Because they knew that a life void of passion was not a life lived fully and authentically. Passion and authenticity go hand in hand, and thus make love and loyalty possible. That brings us back to the question I began with, which is: What do those nonexistent entities know about faith or love or loyalty? And the answer is: It really doesn't matter. What matters is what *we* know and whether or not we're willing to live true to what we know, remaining loyal to our dreams, visions, and understanding of this amazing life that we've been given.

Belief Systems and Carbon Emissions

✳   ✳   ✳

On a sweltering day such as today, it's far too easy to get all caught up in a string of unpleasant thoughts and predictions about the possible perils of climate change. I could fall into that swirling sea effortlessly enough; it is really freaking hot today – triple-digit temperatures for nearly a week. It's not easy to laugh out loud while the earth is heating up. Our earth's core has always been on fire; it's been ablaze from the beginning – just as hot as the surface of our sun, most scientists and geologists agree.

Although we do not live on the sun, we do live and hopefully thrive as a result of it. As far as we know, no one has ever built a summer home or winter cottage in or near the actual core of our truly miraculous planet. I think it fair to say that most of us would like to help build a home or cottage in the molten center of our divine planet – a place of permanent warmth and shelter for a few special people we know. Yet logic and reason continue to tell us that in spite of our noble ideas and altruistic desires, any such construction is impossible.

At this point in time it remains crucial for us to focus on what is truly possible. But human beings can't seem to agree on what is actually feasible, or to see eye to eye on what constitutes reality. We agree to disagree far too easily and all too often if you ask me, simply concurring that reality is subjective.

We have a seemingly wide range of archaic and post-modern beliefs, many of which have been designed to help us obliterate the burden of logic and reason – beliefs that insist upon or strongly encourage blind obedience, the malignant array of hierarchical systems that force their followers "for the sake of faith" to lift a sacred stick from hallowed ground and poke it into their eye of intuition, vowing never to trust their own thoughts or feelings again from that day forward. If and when doubt or confusion of any kind raise their heads, they simply turn to their malevolent leaders and ask them what is right, what is wrong, and what is real; because they have taken an oath – an irrational vow never to trust their own judgment.

Therein lies the challenge of any collective focus for the purpose of determining what is possible. Feasibility is repeatedly hampered by belief in blind obedience; viable ideas for healthy and practical change are routinely disregarded by those who vehemently insist: God is on *our* side, and *not* on yours!

Beliefs such as these would best be used for compost. They would be useful as fertilizer for billions of plants, flowers, and fruit trees – trees that provide us with necessary food and oxygen in exchange for all the excess carbon created by faulty belief systems that only add to the dangers in relation to climate change.

Standing Beneath the Piquant Canopy

✳   ✳   ✳

This fruitful darkness looks like a crimson chimney atop the stony mystery of all these collective prophesies. Upon my long, true, wooden table of artful intervention there is a teacup set for any insightful guest who wants to join me and inspire me while I write. It's a beautiful cup, by the way – midnight on the outside, with fourteen-carat gold leaf trim around the inspired edges – and on the inside... infinite ivory.

Beyond these earthy placemats with traces of food from the ongoing feast – including a few seeds left from yesterday's bread; beyond the dusty ground that Don Quixote and I have kneeled upon more times than I can even remember; beyond those Spanish heat clouds, ten miles east of a kind of purgatory where reluctant prophets stop to explore their weaknesses and find their strengths, by virtue of embracing both – I've stopped beyond those imaginative markers a number of times myself, if truth be told. And because I went there willingly, with several tender nerves exposed, I'm able to make appropriate distinctions between viable visions and untenable fantasies, between the dreams that beg for illustration and honest expression – for the sake of being undeniably actualized, since chimerical imagery may sooth a troubled mind, though only momentarily.

Many well-known teachers and notable sages are only half right, if that, at least some of the time – something that any true seeker really ought to know. Beyond the smokescreen of smoldering improbabilities lies the teal blue mystic sea of lively consequence – the sea that no one enters into by chance or happenstance; there are no exceptions made for philosophers, prophets, teachers, sages, or solar-powered poets like the one I've become.

If and when you stand before that sea, you will see and bear witness to the hand of fate while watching the waves of destiny. And even then you may be feeling too intimidated to jump in and start to swim. If you weren't, you wouldn't be there in the first place. Who wouldn't have some degree of trepidation while watching the waves of their own destiny? Who wouldn't quiver a little while standing alone on the quiet shore of their enlivened awareness, compelled by the hand of fate making waves in the teal blue mystic sea.

I remember the first time I stood there shivering in the warmth of pure awareness wherein my fearful trembling turned into pulsating ecstasy, sometimes called "the quickening." It takes time to learn to sit or stand still inside the tipi of divine temptation, knowing you're about to burst. It takes time for us to honor our own primal urges and swim freely in the waters of that mystic sea. It requires courage and relentless commitment to really float in those waters without getting bloodied by the jagged rocks that line the shores of our co-creative destinies, or to stand poised on a perpendicular precipice of compelling possibilities, one balanced carefully upon another. It takes courage to maintain our composure at the edges of our world, standing beneath the piquant canopy of continuous color, at the quixotic summit of our deepest, truest thoughts, with the soles of our feet touching the dust that settled upon that vibrant pinnacle while we collected all we needed to paint our world with the emotion of enlightened plausibility.

The Sound of Coastal Fog

※　※　※

I'm standing alone near a muted sea with waves that can be heard, though barely seen. I consider this a flawless morning, with fog so thick that sea and sky are utterly indistinguishable – a seemingly solid silver-blue expression of mystical connectedness with a touch of pink and intermittently playful streaks of orange.

It's far too easy for us to miss the perfection of a morning such as this, without skyline to be seen, or horizon to focus on or sail toward. If we feel the need for stark distinction or colorful contrast, it's up to us to create it or imagine it – which are fundamentally the same thing – because what we miss while wishing for clear, bright skies on pristinely clouded mornings is the misty invitation for us to imagine.

Standing here, now, in these cream-colored sands, listening to the primordial roar of a sea that can't be seen through this three-dimensional wall of coastal fog, is an invitation too compelling to ignore. If I didn't know better, I might start to imagine that the voracious roar of this timeless sea is being produced, directed, and fully orchestrated by the spirit of rolling fog – fog that seems inseparable from the waves that can't be seen. By virtue of shear inseparability, I must conclude, or at least consider the low clouds and fog now rushing forward with antediluvian grace and fluidity to be a faithful part of the sound I'm hearing now.

We all know about thunderclouds and the crashing sounds they're capable of making. But until today, I had never heard the roaring sounds of floating fog, rushing clouds, and invisible waves. Or if I had, I was largely, if not entirely unaware of it, or all too willing to accept it as something else. Today I won't deny what my senses tuned in to, nor will I explain away the imaginative insights made available to me through intuition. I heard the roar of floating fog, and it was as calming as those waves we love to listen to.

I've taken it in and done my best to convey it to you in real time, which in my estimation is timeless – as timeless as a thundercloud or bolt of lightning; timeless as a verdant hillside, peppered with an array of wild-flowers; timeless as a love song sung from the center of a well-healed heart that needed to be broken for the sake of knowing every side if love; time-less as a fraternal whisper carried by the wind, or a broken branch turned into driftwood through an organic urge to carry the mystery further; timeless as the magic that children want to steal from the glowing bellies of fireflies – the intermittent luminescence used in airy courtship rituals that something within us knows we're going to need. Even in our precious days of playful innocence, the glowing things that cannot last call out to us.

The essence or soul of what we are is drawn to shiny things. We feel inspired to reach toward things that sparkle, like those jewels in the eyes of true human beings that in our most natural state we feel compelled to look into in order to discover what we need. We want to seize the glow and serve the light simultaneously, and I fervidly believe we have the power to do both.

Squeezing the Seeds of an Ongoing Understanding

✳   ✳   ✳

Beneath the burnt orange cover of my current notebook there is a paradise waiting to be found. After a dozen years of daily practice, of ritual and contemplation, it seems to be the perfect time for me to extract the artful essence of my endless sentences in order to seize the heart of my quintessential soul. I want to capture it for the sake of greater expansion – for the ultimate act of freedom: liberation through creative and impassioned expression. One might think that after all this time it would be easy, like trimming roses, or the ever-popular proverbial walk in the park. And sometimes it is, though there are other times it seems more like walking barefoot over shards of broken glass – a painful, bloody, disconcerting mess.

Fortunately, I've experienced fewer of those times than most romantics might imagine. More often than not, it feels like walking nearly naked across soft sands – a jovial stroll along the open road with some sharp stones to beware of and the occasional rattlesnake to listen for, take notice of, and then walk around respectfully.

When we manage to keep our eyes and ears open and aligned with our hearts, there tends to be an endless stream of lively, colorful, musical surprises, such as silhouettes of sandhill cranes soaring through a fiery autumn sky like robust brush strokes on a twilight blue canvas.

I never tire of all the scintillating contrasts of color, shade, and lively shadow, such as quivering cactus rising from a dew-covered, night-frosted desert landscape while pink-ivory clouds create the ideal doorway for those auspicious beams of light. Those are among the endless gifts I refuse to take for granted – the exotic/quixotic nature of creative exhilaration.

There seems to be an incessant urge for artful self-discovery – a perpetual longing for the source of all things sacred. We all learn, whether we wish to or not, that things aren't always what they seem – people in particular, much of the time. As long as those lessons don't completely overwhelm us, we can distinguish the many things that aren't as they seem from those that are – a crucial distinction that must be made repeatedly.

As for that incessant urge I mentioned above... that remains precisely and profoundly as it seems. How we respond to the urge for artful self-discovery and how we opt to express it keeps the creative process as infinite and individual as the primal urge itself.

And so it has come to this – the perfect time for me to squeeze the seeds of my true understanding, allowing the healing oil held within them to be holistically released.

Putting It All in Perspective
Again and Again

※　　※　　※

If I simply decide to do this one more time – to sit and say what's on my mind – maybe then I'll have the whole thing in perspective. But the whole thing keeps changing all the time, so whatever perspective I manage to get it all into is bound to be different tomorrow.

No matter how many times I sit down to say what's true for me now, it could never be enough; I could never say it all or come close to telling the entire story of my life, let alone the utterly endless story of the whole wide world.

And I need to remember to remember that I'm not meant to. Then when the urge to say it all takes hold, I'll be able to check it. When I feel compelled to put the whole thing in perspective, I'll remember that perspective is a lot like weather. Then I can immerse myself in the moment at hand and find the meaning in that, because at the beginning, middle, and end of the day, that's what it comes down to: the meaning we discover in the moments that make up our lives.

I don't feel compelled to write my memoirs at this stage of my life, and I don't know if I ever will. I don't imagine the world to be in dire need of my astonishing autobiography. I believe it needs my poetry and the insights gained through honest reflection a great deal more; those I wish to make fully accessible and as widely available as possible.

I can't disregard the day-to-day dynamic of steady change. Nor do I wish to undermine the importance of giving my fullest attention to the one and only moment at hand, wherein all the available co-creative energy resides.

That's what I tap in to each and every time I face the empty page and make a fresh commitment to fill it with something simple, something lively, or something poetically surreal. Who I become in the process turns out to be more important than anything I could say.

I need to come here – I need to be here – where all the co-creative energy resides. This is where I come to shape the destiny that quintessentially shapes me.

My One and Only Hour

* * *

If I had only one hour in which to say it all, I would immediately dismiss my sense of being overwhelmed and begin by saying Amen! Why not start at the end of the prayer I've been living nearly all my life, knowing all the while it's the middle? Every end is a beginning, and every beginning comes with a built-in conclusion to the illusion of every end.

If I had but one lonely hour in which to say it all, I would say: Thank you... plain, simple, and sincere. In the time remaining in my only hour, I might then wish to mention the great tree of life, which is any tree you take the time to truly notice and really look at: oak, cypress, cherry, apple, plum, or evergreen. I would say: Thank you for all the fruit I managed to find throughout my lifetime, for all those juicy peaches, delicious pears, and golden-ripe pineapples, and the sweet purple, green, or sienna-red grapes that I've savored alone on hilltops, and the fruit shared with friends, lovers, and familiar strangers who seemed like long-lost members of my family, and for simply holding my wife and our two amazing sons in the robust center of my enlivened awareness. My heart and soul would spontaneously start to sing the song that represents my deepest truth, and every cell of my being would be bathed in the healing frequency of sacred sound.

If I had only one hour in which to say everything, I would say: Love is the ultimate purpose of human existence. I have lived that purpose more fully, freely, deeply, and completely than most men ever dare to even dream about.

And in that first, last, and only hour of perfect existence – in that instant that by nature holds the vibrant energy that flows through time to the eyes and ears of the final hour wherein the untainted energy of pure light and love kisses the final, lonely, only hour upon the mouth of infinite possibility and starts the whole world over again – I would express my eternal gratitude for the fundamental blessings of all the arts. If god is anything at all, nothing whatsoever, or everything and nothing flawlessly combined, in my mind god is, and shall forever remain, the ultimate artist.

Any true creator of something meaningful is inextricably connected with the infinite, with or without a fixed belief in a real or well-imagined deity. In my one and only hour of true existence, I wouldn't waste one precious minute believing, because I'd be far too busy *being*! I wouldn't want to squander one single second clinging to a fixed idea that hadn't grown from the tree of life within.

In my one and only hour of exquisite existence, I would write or speak my final poem and drink a toast to all the sacred words that ever lived within me. And at the end of the poem that is my living prayer I would sing my first and last Amen, kiss the final hour upon the open mouth of infinite possibility, and start the whole world over again...

I Can Tell

✳   ✳   ✳

I can tell that the world is shifting, though I don't know if I'll find anything more solid than sentiment to allow me to tell you how. Then again,
that could be just enough for both of us. All I can do is offer my thoughts
openly, without any erratic editing or resistance to what wishes to come
through.

The winds are expressing their wild side today, and, I must say, I like
it. After all, *I* can be sunny, warm, and wild all at once. Why be less than
whole if you can help it? Why hold back while the world is shifting, even
when sentiment tends to remain your steady guide? Be grateful for all
the forces that are willing to guide you, even when they come cloaked in
raw emotion.

Sentiment isn't something for us to frown upon or nonchalantly
discount as it begins to rise and swell and shape our views from the inside. Without it we would be as motionless as a bronze or marble statue.
We are moved by what we're willing and able to feel, not merely think.
There is *motion* in emotion, don't forget. Without sentiment, comprised
of thought and feeling, we'd be hard-pressed to form an opinion or shape
a philosophy that permits us to express ourselves in any genuine manner

at all. Nor would we know anything about empathy or true compassion, without which human beings might still technically exist, but without the slightest chance of ever actualizing our humanity.

The shift we need and want and continue to wish for is toward the humanity we've yet to fully see. We've had many marvelous glimpses – memorable moments and magnificent instances of kindness, creativity, and inspired action. Only now we need to see it on a worldwide scale, through an uncompromising commitment to being our best on every level. Anything less would be akin to placing a child-like colorful cartoon Band-Aid over a badly infected self-inflicted wound.

We need to eradicate the widely accepted epidemic of political insincerity funded by corporations such as Bechtel, Halliburton, Monsanto, Exxon Mobile, Fox, G.E., and Coca-Cola, to mention but a few. They have created a collective contagion while continuing to make billions of dollars pretending to cure the ills they willfully caused.

It's time to embrace the triumphant winds of creative revision – those that fill the sails that help propel those magnanimous ships that continue to race toward the discovery and implementation of healthy, productive, and viable change.

How Far?

✳   ✳   ✳

How far are we really willing to go to find, affirm, and bring to life the dreams that dwell within us? That remains one of the questions worth asking time and again. It needs to be asked repeatedly, because the moment we step into the awareness of one potent dream, another one emerges immediately.

The instant we touch the edge of one true objective, we begin seeding some of the aspirations that seemed beyond our senses a moment before; fresh reflections flood forth like sunlight after a week of steady rain.

Then we begin to reconcile the fantasies of our present with the illusions of our past. If we stay focused long enough, we start to pacify the many untenable hallucinations that do not serve us. Little by little, we cross the threshold that leads to the absence of time, or timelessness – a kind of holiday away from the ticking clocks that keep us on time, though all too typically out of touch with the dreams that dwell within us.

Once we cross the Rubicon, there is no turning back, or even looking back at the world in the same way. Once we've taken a willful sabbatical from the many popular perceptions of where we all are and what we've grown into, thinking for ourselves becomes possible. If we're courageous enough to stick with it a while, we are bound to reinvent ourselves in the process.

Through creative juxtaposition and intoxicating paradox we learn to broaden and boldly color our perceptions. We don't invent new shades per se; we simply mix what's fully present, and then observe the world with a fresh coat of radiant paint. It isn't as if we don't have a hand in it – or two hands, for that matter. It's simply that we can't create a single thing that in some sense hasn't been here from the beginning.

So we rearrange time, mix our own colors, and move in unity with what we wish to see, reinventing ourselves in the process and giving birth to what we know we need to be. Then we can stand in the shadow of a well-rooted oak knowing that the sacred spirit of such an astonishing tree really does live within us. Or do what I did yesterday while standing between two towering rows of slowly swaying cypress trees: I stuck my hand, then half my arm, inside the deep, green, fertile mystery of the tree that I stood closest to, and to my delight and great surprise, a dove emerged from the emerald womb of that lively, well-rooted entity, circled twice above my head, then flew away.

I hadn't been able to see inside the branches I felt urged to reach into, though I had an undeniable sense that something was there. And when that dove appeared from within the middle branches, my feeling was confirmed. We live in the shelter of our own individual mystery much of the time – the splendiferous womb of our ever-emerging dreams.

In Honor of the Never-Ending Feast

I sit alone watching wax melt slowly beneath the heat of a steady flame, my rustic candle standing tall in the center of my table – a tiny flame, though bold enough to stand alone and bright enough to challenge any intermittent darkness. I sit alone at the very same table that held a joyful feast the night before – a blissful banquet shared with family and friends. This now semi-empty table was covered from end to end with plates of hearty, delicious, meticulously prepared food – two grand platters, three exquisite serving bowls, forks, knives, spoons, and cotton napkins. We dined on blessed food – delicious food I won't describe right now. We ate, we drank, and we talked and laughed and celebrated the extraordinary wonders of real life – family, friends, and plenty of food – with music playing quietly enough to invite conversation and permit the rich life, which is real life, to prevail.

The fundamental meaning of my own true everyday lives within the things I keep coming back to – the crucial, artful, inspiring things that feed my spirit, nurture my body, fuel my psyche, and give my soul a sensual massage. Now I sit alone at my dining room table – the horizontal host of countless feasts – with my rustic candle standing in the middle. I sit alone savoring the richness of my honest memories – fresh, lively, and every bit as sumptuous as the food we feasted on last night.

I blend all that is before me now with the unspoiled richness of what went before – a delightful puree of past and present, exquisitely balanced and perfectly spiced with two fresh whole cloves of creative fantasy and mixed with the unstrained juice of prophetic imagery that can and shall be savored at the proper time. I sit alone, though not alone, at an anything-but-empty table, tasting thoughts and savoring memories blended with visions, dreams, and fantasies of what is still to come.

And I will say this now without needless doubt or hesitation: I am a healthy, grateful, well-fed poet, father, husband, and man of my own time, living within the dream of my own making. From the ashes of at least a thousand burnt offerings I have managed to build something meaningful – something true and very beautiful. I say this from the joyful fullness of my heart and soul: I am as grateful as any man who has ever really lived the life he was given. I am humbled by the splendor that surrounds me and encouraged by the mystery and majesty that abounds. And I don't believe in accidental wonderment; there is no such thing as nonchalant enchantment – no half-hearted astonishment, haphazard breakthroughs, or chance encounters that help align you with destiny. And there is no possibility of inadvertent enlightenment. Real enlightenment requires free thinking, and thinking freely requires steady discipline and systematic, sacred practice. Celebration, on the other hand, can be spontaneous – full, complete, and instantaneous – the moment we manage to see the world as it is.

In Honor of the Sacred Fermentation

※　※　※

It may rain sometime later today, and I really don't mind. This moist, balmy air is refreshing to my skin, my psyche, and my soul. I may drink pine needle tea in the late afternoon, and then pick bundles of ripe, black, shimmering elderberries, and begin the new batch of wine. And when the magic of time mixes thoroughly with these hand-picked berries, causing the perfect fermentation to take place, I will have one more reason among the many to celebrate.

In the meantime, I will celebrate the scent, color, and lively sounds massaging my senses as I write; perfect fermentation cannot be rushed. Don't be afraid to sleep deeply when you need to, or nap beneath the spirited branches of elder trees or human beings who offer shelter to those who feel in need of it. Good wine can't be hurried, hastened, or persuaded in any way by our impatience, any more than we can become elders a moment sooner than we're meant to, though aging alone provides no guarantee that we will become the elders others need. Hang around long enough and you'll get older; we all do. But we don't all become the elders that we could be – the wise ones people look to for answers and guidance. It sometimes seems as if the elders we need are in danger of becoming extinct.

We've all been taught, conditioned, and continually hypnotized into expecting little more than aches, pains, and the lessening of nearly all of our natural abilities as we get older. No wonder we're hard-pressed to find true elders in this day and age – an age in which we're programmed to dread getting any older at all. We've forgotten how, or never learned to fully honor the natural, sacred, and empowering process of consciously aging. Instead we keep attempting to stop it altogether – to bring the great organic splendor of actively aging to a false, defiant, and cosmetically or surgically aided halt! And we seem to succeed at halting the inherent wisdom that comes with aging when we honor it from within a society that shares a commercialized mindset perpetuated by the latest and greatest newly discovered fictitious fountain of youth – a society that produces olders ill-equipped to be our elders.

Where are the old ones beaming with passionate wisdom hard-earned through a long life truly lived – the ones we find in stories, myths, and those epic poems that help guide us? We've turned fact into fiction, and heroic fantasy into the horrors of everyday life. We dismiss the beauty, power, and wisdom found in world mythology and turn the most compelling truths into the pale, insipid fiction of our day, while clinging tenaciously to the wildly implausible fairy tales that we call the gospel. We place fear-based fabrications atop the tallest man-made pedestals and teach children of all ages not to question them. Each and every day graves are filled with those who never truly lived – those who refused to question or examine the life-draining lies they attempted to live with. And thus the well-lived life is considered to be an anomaly; nearly any well-rounded, joyful life lived fully and authentically tends to be seen as an artful aberration.

Nevertheless and ever-the-more, this is the life I continue to choose for myself – a blessed deviation from what is treated like and accepted as the norm. Perfect, natural fermentation cannot be rushed in order to quicken the completion of the wine I started making long before I left the womb. I will not spoil the exquisite taste and sacred bouquet that only patience and proper time is able to produce. I am committed to making the most deliciously uplifting, creatively intoxicating wine the world has ever tasted – a fresh, unique, and precious vintage guaranteed to make even Dionysus envious – a delightfully irresistible beverage my many muses will share with me in endless celebration. We will lift our clear blue crystal goblets and drink a heart-felt toast to the poet who prevailed!

More than One Way to Tell

✳   ✳   ✳

I could tell you that the waves of Maroussi are still breaking wildly at the shores of my awareness, and who could really argue otherwise without first being part of the awareness that allows me to tell you anything at all? The pine trees I see from my window are all aglow with morning dew, and I am eager to consume these glistening instances in their entirety, slowly enough to taste the exquisite tenderness unfolding before me and savor these salient expressions that are boundless.

I must confess that my desire to remain unnaturally linear was lost a long time ago. I don't miss it. Nor do I intend to organize a search party for the sake of retrieving what I never really wanted in the first place. I prefer to move as nature intended, like the winds and waves and words of emancipated poets. In other words, I wish to move and think and act as freely as one can without neglecting the responsibility built in to such a privilege.

When we observe the movements of the natural world, we see that they are typically cyclical and circular, like the seasons. I want to move the way winter moves and melds and organically surrenders to spring, while reserving my creative right to skip backward when I wish to from any auspicious autumn to a particularly memorable spring. Or to leap from my boyhood in the metropolitan Midwest – from that well-known, windy city in the state of Illinois – to those ancient, treasured, and often chaotic landscapes of the war-torn Middle East. I have lived and thrived for a period of time in both of these middle regions of our world.

I could tell you that The Lions of Delos are still roaring, and that those ancient redwoods in Northern California are standing taller than ever. I could tell you that I learned to walk the day before yesterday, after crawling across our floors the day before. I could tell you that my spine has been strengthened by a sacred stone placed upon my ailing back by the gentle, loving hand of a living angel. And I could tell you that everything I've said today is true! Every deliberately chosen, consciously selected word is reverberating with the essence of my own spirited understanding.

I do know how to tell a story in step-by-step, meticulous detail. I am fully capable of providing thoughts, facts, and information in the straightforward, time-honored, stylistic tradition. I do know how to do that when I need to, though I learned to do it even better after tearing down those poetic fence posts pounded into the ground long ago by men I've never met, thus allowing my deep, personal, poetic expressions to run freely through those colorful fields of illustrious prose – better at least from my perspective, and I do hope from the reader's as well. In any case, this is my way, my style, my mythologically guided methodology – a creative way of telling truthful stories from the glorious inside-out.

I could tell you that on Thanksgiving Day – my long-time favorite holiday – I was hit by a train of discontented consciousness while standing naked in the shower, and I was barely able to step out of the shower, open the bathroom door, and quickly lower myself to the floor, because the intense pain in my lower back insisted that I could no longer stand. Later that day, or early that night, I rediscovered the miraculous skill of crawling – a skill that got me from my bed to the bathroom, and for which I was exceedingly grateful. I was able to crawl without excruciating pain. I could move without involuntary spasms of nerve-compressed agony sending shock waves through the physical, mental, and emotional body of a universal man.

And I can tell you that I am more than merely on the mend; I am mended and miraculously renewed. I am sitting, walking, dancing, soaring, and, as always… writing in my own way.

In Response to Hearing Footsteps in Mid-July

❋　❋　❋

I rush toward those footsteps I keep hearing below my window – footsteps provoking other footsteps – the stimulus of human feet creating a slip-sliding, sauntering rhythm as they glide across the ground.

Now I'm seated again at my table, strolling over pale blue lines with my silver-tipped Sure-Grip pen. This is where I walk… and skip, dance, leap, and sometimes fly. I come here to flee the world and find it simultaneously. I come here to test the waters of my world – to swim and occasionally drown – only to be miraculously resuscitated by a breathy thought that offers buoyancy, or saved by some successive sound, note, chord, or sublime interval of precious silence.

Then I lift my head and open my eyes to endless wonder. I take a deep, slow, deliberate breath, and then take notice of the blood-red leaves on my summer plum trees. Then, while sipping my morning coffee, the many complex abstracts immediately make sense to me. Either that or I have a knack for finding comfort in artful things that seem nonsensical at first glance, allowing me to feel at ease with the incomprehensible – an invaluable tool for those of us who are alive and well and still living in the world.

In any case, I find it refreshing – a faithful leap into what could be called *exquisite equilibrium* – into erratic, if not eternal equanimity, akin to bathing in a pristine stream in late July near the bridge that we'll come to later as we continue to harvest our very best collective thoughts while a billion monarch butterflies make their maiden voyage.

In the meantime I sit here at my table saying this because it's this or nothing at all, and I find this a lot more interesting. It's up to me to personify some of the weighty things so that we might lighten up enough to fly and breathe new life into some of the semi-lifeless stones. It's up to me to lift the fallen pine cones when I find them on the ground after a wind storm; to carry them home in order to tap in to their fertility. It's up to me to put my world in perfect order, remaining cool within the chaos and making sense out of the abstracts.

If only we could make a living caring deeply for our world... that would really be something! Maybe then my sweet Sophia wouldn't look so sad. If only I could make a substantial living as the poet that I am. Maybe then Aphrodite would be born again from Pacific, as opposed to Aegean, sea foam, fully formed on the Malibu shore, with the intent and burning desire to have lunch with me in order to lure me into an ever-deeper connection with my world. Maybe then some of my sleeping passions would be awakened, allowing me to touch the world directly and be touched back. Maybe then Mnemosyne would urge me to fully remember who I am and what I need to do. Perhaps the mother of the many muses would persuade me with her rhyme and rhythm to freely and robustly follow my own – to tap even deeper into the source of what I feel compelled to express. And maybe Persephone would kiss my cheek, lips, eyes, and forehead before returning once again to the underworld, leaving me with an array of irrepressible insights into the Eleusinian mysteries, spellbound by her innocent, albeit majestic beauty and a yearning for her footsteps in the spring.

Beginning with the Pause

✳   ✳   ✳

I need to begin with a simple pause… one that may or may not be pregnant, though fertile without a doubt. Let me start there – with this inventive delay – because I don't know where else to spring from but the present.

From this sacred respite I make my leap into the mystery, which is the moment that gives nourishment to all our living mythology. I wrap myself in what is scantly known and name it splendor. Yesterday I called it elegance, while watching sunlit waves break on ancient rocks. And the week before I called it winter, while watching wildflowers implode and turn to dust to feed the ground that gave them time to pronounce their prolific color.

A decade ago I called this realization, as I recognized the destiny that is my own while embracing the awareness it continued to offer me – wholeheartedly. Creativity is the essence of every epiphany; I've had many, without a doubt, each one adding a fresh dimension to the one that came before.

And I have, on a number of occasions, carried an eagle feather into that cave of contemplation, because I was seeking soaring thoughts. Not the answers, necessarily, obvious or otherwise, but simply thoughts I could connect with, listen to like music, and dance with in those inevitable moments of darkness. I've gone into that cave untold times – to retreat, to reflect upon the beguiling mystery, or to resurrect the dream of my beginning. I've entered in to retrieve the memories that remain pertinent and purposeful – those that permit me to recreate the moment at hand and reconstruct myself in the process.

All these tender recreations could feed into the illusion that life is nothing but ecstasy and perpetual bliss; nerves be damned, and may any thought or emotion that suggests anything otherwise be muted, dissolved, incinerated, obliterated, denied, and then renamed. Though that may appease us momentarily, it always fails to serve us in the long run. It doesn't really matter what we opt to call it in the long run. What matters is how we choose to respond to it, whether contradiction wears a baseball cap, or hubris is topped with a cowboy hat, or hypocrisy comes cloaked in a velvet robe and a jewel-encrusted crown. Denial has an extensive wardrobe, and delusion comes in an array of styles. And yet both are pretty naked much of the time, especially when fully dressed in their Sunday best.

Now let us get back to ecstasy, at least momentarily, because any life lived fully must know bliss, which is never outside the realm of mystery but is, in fact, the living heart of it. If we refuse the rapture of day-to-day life, why should we expect it to greet us at the end of an unlived story? Euphoria runs through the bloodstream of actualized life. Bliss is the erotic pulse within the living, breathing mystery – the perpetually robust riddle of real life. Elation fuels the dreams that direct the true life of the soul, which we tend not to move toward until we think we've suffered enough.

We find our inspiration in the darkness as well as in the light, like the unseen energy dancing on and beneath the surface of those balmy shadows that lie naked and exposed on the frozen tundra, melting through the ice and snow. Or like a fig leaf floating on the murky surface of a mystical lake near the end of August, a month of romance in a seemingly endless season of true love (or pure lust – an undeniable impulse either way – the force that urges roses to bloom and our hearts and souls and psyches to open fully), while rowboats float over deep, green waters, passing glistening lily pads kissing the mystical surface, leaving me to wonder what's beneath.

What might we see – what might we realize if we were to open our eyes fully in this great womb of life? I could tell you, though I doubt it would do any good. I could describe it in vivid detail, but unless you have your own point of reference, my depiction could be rendered worthless – or worse. I could tell you what I saw before my eyes were open, though that might be entirely pointless. However, I will tell you that what I saw before and after I entered the womb is much the same as what I'm seeing now; I was searching for my beginning – then and now – and opted to honor the pause.

Beyond Belief

※　※　※

Evergreens paint opaque shadows on the rooftops across the way. On a motionless morning near the midpoint of November, I find it easy enough to almost believe this moment has been frozen in the fluid of true, eternal time, though there's no need to believe what I see and what I know. There's no need to believe in the gentle wind – the amiable breeze that inspires the supple limbs of an elegant pine to move like lively, shining emeralds dropped into a teal-blue-tinted crystal bowl filled with golden primordial honey.

There's no need to believe in what we see, or what we fail to see, for that matter. Knowing is enough – when we really know – though when we don't, believing can be useful to a point. To what point?… that we must determine for ourselves.

It's up to us to claim our quiet moments and then opt to declare them spotless! Then we can seize the feasibility of living within only the immaculate instances of our own robust existences. Once again I remind myself and anyone else who wishes to listen that we need not believe in the unblemished moments of our lively, light-filled awareness in order to be in them.

Some say seeing is believing, and I can comprehend the logic of such a statement, though after seeing and believing lies the potential for being – beyond the need to believe. Belief can be taught with the aid of doctrine, story, or dusty credo printed onto pages made from wood pulp or carved into cold, lifeless stone. Being, on the other hand, does not require any fixed ideology or tendentious tenet in order to be divinely credible and fully accessible at the same time. In other words, direct awareness doesn't require dogma, which is built in to most disturbingly rigid systems of belief.

On a mid-November morning as balmy as this one, I find it easy enough to almost believe that if there is a genuine Garden of Eden, this is it, and I am in it, though I have no need to believe what I already know, which is that this is it, and I am of it, as well as in it.

Direct awareness does not require us to cling to any particular maxims, precepts, or convenient canons turned into unholy emblems of contempt. Dogma, on the other hand, does. Direct awareness inspires a faithful kind of courageous letting go. Belief, by contrast, tends to encourage tenacious clinging to a less than inspirational list of forgone conclusions, along with the less than lively tendency to deny ourselves the splendiferous fullness of the immediate moment.

Direct awareness, within the fullness of being, does not insinuate, intimate, or imply. It simply is! And what a profoundly beautiful simplicity we get to witness, and be part of, when we're in it.

Messy

✳ ✳ ✳

Creativity is not always
Neat and clean, in fact it's
Often very messy… like childbirth.

I watched my two sons
Come into the world…

The pink-red, yellow-brown liquids
That flowed before them—that miraculous,
Colorful wet arrival, followed quickly by
The afterbirth.

Then the diapers, the drool,
The projectile vomit I was baptized
With, just as I stepped out of the shower.

The thrown food, muddy shoes,
Torn clothes, bloody knees, juice stains
In every room – on the carpet, chairs, and sofa…

My boys, above all else, remain the
Greatest mess I've ever gotten into!

The Ecstatic Pain of Steady Birth

※　　※　　※

There is simply no way for us to finish what we lack the courage or the vision to begin. It's all too easy to wrap ourselves in discontentment and pretend we're really trying, as if being overwhelmed and lacking happiness is substantial proof of our great efforts, or that the weighty angst we carry with us is a sure sign of our sincerity.

Though if we really look, we cannot help but see the attachment human beings have to their suffering. It seems to be the favorite pastime of many people I know. You probably know them too, or you may even be one of them. I'm not referring to the inevitable suffering that comes with living a full life. "There is no individuation without suffering," Carl Jung said. I hated hearing that quote for the first time, decades ago, while I was in my early twenties. I already knew what suffering was, and I really didn't want to know it any better. I wasn't eager for more. I was, however, eager to discover who I am – my fate, my path, my character. I wanted nothing more than to follow my path faithfully, albeit without the suffering Jung said would be necessary.

These days I can smile with a deeper understanding of my own – an understanding derived from suffering, numbness, and bliss. And I can say that bliss remains the preeminent guide I follow along this path that is my own. I have suffered, survived, and thus built the character necessary to walk this path I recognize as my own. I understand the relationship between individuation and suffering to be one part of the whole of any full life – a portion, period, or periodic timeframe of any actualized life.

There is, however, a fundamental difference between honoring a portion of the whole that includes heartache, pain, and emotional distress, and making suffering so significant that it becomes the whole of your life. The latter is not at all what Jung was suggesting, nor am I.

And now I feel compelled to tell you that words have not been flying out like endless rain into a paper cup these last few weeks. Hence the urge to borrow a wonderful line from Lennon, ever so slightly paraphrased. There have been a number of days in recent weeks when I haven't written at all. I suppose I could borrow a little more from that marvelous song and simply say, "They slither while they pass, they slip away across the universe."

There is this shift in my creative process that could well be but another pregnant pause. In fact, it must be! I feel too full of thoughts and dreams and lofty visions for this to be anything less than that. What trimester is this? What's my due date? And what might I be giving birth to this time? Fraternal twins from the seeds of different myths – two books born with different features, one with brown eyes, one with blue? I know their names already. I've known their names for several years now, conceived within the womb of my awareness. I am with child again – an expectant father and grateful man who carries the seeds of creative life within the womb of collective consciousness – a writer, poet, author-in-love with the full creative process. Sometimes I feel the pressure, pangs, and kicks that come from within. And sometimes I get heartburn from the low PH of new life – the natural, necessary, periodically painful chemistry that stems from the eagerness carried inside us.

Eager to See

※　※　※

I'm eager to see what spills out onto these vacant pages once the chalice of neglected innocence is turned entirely upside down. How could one not wonder what will spill out after all this time – century after century of self-repressed rapture – while the stars that matter most to us remain in place; while children play and parents continue to mar and manipulate the pristinely open minds of their eager offspring? The results of those manipulations turn out to be less than good a great deal of the time, and still they seem so surprised by all the confusion they unconsciously create.

They continue to dream of endless fortune, yet foster mostly what they consider foul – the odious misfortune that their dreadful misconceptions give birth to every hour on the hour. But tell them they have more than one hand in the shaping of their destinies and watch their eyes glaze over before they close, whereat it's probably best that you walk away. You might as well, because there's little to no chance that you'll be heard.

Better to stroll alone along the cobblestones, talking to or singing for yourself. Those old stones are much better listeners than those who shut their eyes and ears to what you wish to offer open-heartedly – far, far better than any of those typical manipulators.

And though I may note the wretched cries and forlorn whispers I hear in passing, they're not the voices that I turn to or rely upon for counsel. I may not disregard them instantaneously – I listen, and then release them into the wilds of the collective mind. It isn't as if I ignore the forlorn or turn a deaf ear to the steadily dejected. I listen deeply – deeply enough to know when it's best to let them go. I let them in and then release them back into the wild, thus allowing them to convene with the broader nature of all living things.

If they're devoured by wolves, so be it. I have more respect for wolves than I do for those habitual manipulators. After all, I've heard them say "dog eat dog" dozens of times. Dog eat dog, wolf eat manipulator – what's the difference? The point is that we all need to eat, and we know it, yet so few know the true joy of the feast.

I'm curious to see what's left once the dust has settled down after the wind storm, though it isn't as if I've worn a blindfold in the meantime, or a mask that does not represent my true nature. Whatever mask I've ever worn, I've made myself. And the older I get, the less I feel the need for any mask at all. My still slightly boyish face reflects the joys and sorrows of a less conventional man – a man who has listened to the vespers of his own soul and taken a chance. The chance I took and continue to take allows me to celebrate my own everyday without restraint.

Everything and Nothing

Aside from the discipline required to get lost each day, I have little – other than a ton of run-on sentences and a thousand or more fascinating stories in various stages of completion. My endless supply of candles isn't endless after all, though I do have more than enough for today. And here I am! Back at the table with my pillar of wax melting slowly beneath the flame.

Call it what you will. But don't neglect to recognize my devotion. Aside from that, I have little. So I keep coming back to what I have – that one little thing that is everything and nothing all at once.

It takes discipline to face that every day – the everything and nothing, inextricably woven into the spirit of my awareness. It requires a unique kind of artful fidelity to my lively psyche, forever unfolding within the infinitely creative soul of my true being.

Aside from that, I'm pretty empty, though it turns out to be the kind of emptiness that creates a vacuum for honest and insightful phrases that beg to be written down. I do my best to facilitate those thoughts that float or fly or fall through space and land within my awareness.

Aside from all those beautiful and auspicious sentences I keep

plucking from thin, though potent air – other than those robust words
that dance like tiny angels along the edges of my psyche – I have little.
Aside from the words I dance with and the light I take in as I lay nearly
naked on rooftops, hilltops, or the sun-soaked sands at the Malibu shore
– other than these, I am nothing, though with them I am everything and
nothing all at once.

The Reverie of Preeminent Possibilities

※　　※　　※

Oceans lead to innocence from where I sit. Boats, bridges, slow-rolling waves – they all come back to the beginning. And in the beginning… well, we get to imagine. In the meantime, I find myself in the middle of all this imagery. Sometimes in the midst of these visions I come face to face with more than a single segment of an extraordinary dream that I recognize as my own – not the once-upon-a-time kind, but the lively, colorful, preeminently irrepressible reverie that refuses to be taken for granted or ignored.

This is where I find myself much of the time – intoxicated by these lofty dreams that have miraculously come to life. Whether I'm sailing freely on a glittering ocean, swimming eagerly in the lake of my youth, or dancing nearly naked like a gentle savage on dry land… I'm alive! And this aliveness is the dream I have allowed. It is the unequivocal collaboration of the coherent collective that has guided me much of the way throughout most of my life thus far.

Even on rainy days such as today, I find the simple comfort, quiet joy, and moist satisfaction of listening to these primal rhythms of steady rain pounding out an endless story upon the round, slightly warped plastic table on my patio. If I were inclined to listen for codes, I'd probably hear one. But instead I hear the unmistakable poetry in everything, which is fully accessible and widely open to anyone attuned to the poiesis of true existence – or the poiesis of one's own process, one might say. Either way, those primal rhythms, like steady rain mixed with pure, unfettered human emotion, run and flow like exquisite rivers of unstoppable light through the canyons of the psyches and the caverns of the souls of those who find a way to stay awake.

Later today, or possibly early this evening, I may decide once again to baptize myself in a rain puddle, or to be soaked to the bone with an understanding that could only prove useful. And days from now, once these rains have ceased, the mud is dry, and dust revisits the changing leaves still clinging to all these autumn trees, I'm bound to remember the rhythm again, because these primal rhythms live inside of me. It all comes back to the beginning, again and again. And in the beginning... well, we get to imagine.

The Sea,
Both Here and There

✳   ✳   ✳

Sometimes the urge to rush forward – without a map or plan or guide-book of any kind – is the only way to go. Sometimes strategy serves only to delay the very thing we say we want and need and tell ourselves we're working toward. Our best laid plans can turn into meticulous procrasti-nation when we talk about a goal incessantly. Sometimes a blueprint for the perfect life becomes a bridle for the spirit that must be free, unfet-tered, and wild enough to know its own aliveness. Whether the bridle is well-made – hand-crafted, stitched to perfection, oiled, shined, and diamond studded – is not the point. Expensive restraints are essentially the same in regard to function as plain, ordinary, everyday bindings of the psyche, spirit, and soul. They restrain us; they impede our thoughts, limit our movements, and ask us to honor hypocrisy.

Shackles are shackles, even though we are repeatedly told that the golden ones are better in every way than those of ordinary iron – one of the many wonders of ironic repetition wherein we witness the world-wide frenzy of overwhelmed souls – desperate, hungry, and thus easy to control, slaving away day after day, hoping to trade their iron chains for chains of gold. And who can blame them? Who can fault them? Who can say that their efforts are entirely void of merit?

The very thought of any forced restriction makes me want to get up and dance immediately! Or light incense near my open window in order to invite my spirited ancestors to dance along with me. These pages are my immortal dance floor – sacred ground on which to tango with the infinite when I wish to, when I care to, when I dare to. This is where my dexterity seems to serve me best by allowing me to continually serve others. I soar across endless pale blue lines like an antelope graced with the glorious wings of an eagle. I sit here now, quiet and still, without restraints or weighty shackles, permitting my pen to dance while my mind wanders and my spirit hovers effortlessly over a rosy sea, kissed and hugged by the resolute glow of this auspicious sunrise.

I know what genuine tenderness is, and it never frightens, confuses, or tempts me to turn away from what I know – what I love and continue to honor. I may not be beyond reproach, though I am patient and passionately autonomous. I may have my list of flaws, though not a single one, or all combined, are enough to rob me of the faith and intuition that compels me to celebrate my own sovereignty. I sit here now without regret or vengeance in my blood. I feel as if I am in steady alignment with the true and appropriate guardians of the soul – my soul – and I consider it enough. It is enough to keep me faithful to the path that is my own – the one that led me to this rosy sea at sunrise without the slightest urge for false confessions or a convoluted desire for reprisal.

And so I move forward through all of these fortunate reflections of my past, gazing eagerly across the sea that is before me, with waves rushing forward without a map or plan or guidebook of any kind, only current, crest, and wave beneath salty, magnetized mist, rising into the source of life itself – into the ethereal clouds from whence they came – back again into that cosmic Camelot, into that kingdom of dreams beyond the Pleiades – light years beyond the Milky Way, past Pegasus and that airy bear eating a galaxy of honey from a heavenly hive, near enough to the Eagle Nebula where embryonic stars are raised on milky light that floods into the universal womb of true existence.

A Metaphoric Dream Well Worth Remembering

✳   ✳   ✳

Sometimes we need to shake the tree of life in order to give new meaning to the morning so that we might have something to carry with us and refer to throughout the day. Sometimes we need to kneel in the dust of a different land in order to find our center, regain our bearings, and remember where we've been. Sometimes walls are turned into doorways when we face them and refuse to be denied.

There are those who seem to be in steady pursuit of some sort of dream, chasing visions, thoughts, and fantasies that may or may not actually be their own. There are others who simply allow themselves to be captured by the spirit of real adventure without the neurotic need or implausible impulse to weigh the velocity of their primal incentives or attempt to measure the barometric pressure of their widely open minds. I understand the primal urge to make our lives meaningful – to give of ourselves, make our marks, and be remembered for our remarkable labors of love. Any sane human being has a natural desire to make a healthy contribution to the world they were born into. How then do we reconcile those deep, undeniable, creative desires with the all-too-typical preoccupation with pointlessness – the mass distraction and sheer futility of attempting to live someone else's life?

Questions like this cannot be answered completely, unequivocally, or once and for all. They need to be answered both individually and repeatedly, each and every time we face a wall and strongly suspect that something meaningful is waiting on the other side. Though we sense, but cannot say precisely what that something is, we know in our souls that it waits and is intended solely for us. Those are the walls that we inevitably come to if and when we choose to follow our destinies faithfully. They are the walls we must face and find a way to get beyond by standing strong and honoring our intuitive refusal to be denied.

Once, in a dream, I watched one of those walls become a doorway. It was a very revealing, deeply moving, memorable metaphor in the making. I was in a large, old, well-established hotel with a history that was palpable, as if the air itself was being oxygenated by lively stories in the midst of being born. I was standing in a hallway adjacent to the hotel lobby on a lively, colorful, newly laid carpet, facing a freshly painted wall, knowing I had been there before and that the wall I was facing had been a doorway the last time I stood there. I knew I was in the right place – the right spot – precisely where I knew I needed to be. I stood there feeling more than a bit perplexed about the freshly painted barricade in front of me – the wall I firmly believed had been a doorway the last time I stood on that spot. I walked up and back a couple of times, searching for the door that wasn't there. Then an elderly gentleman, elegantly dressed and very well groomed, with gray-white hair and a closely trimmed beard and mustache, looked at me and asked, "What's the matter?" I told him exactly what I thought the matter was. I told him that this was where I was supposed to be, that I had been here before, and that the last time I was here there was a door here. This wall was a door! And the well-dressed man looked at me, shook his head, and said in no uncertain terms, "If you know in your heart and soul that there was a door here – that this was a door, as you so clearly stated – THEN TREAT IT LIKE A DOOR AND NOT A WALL!

I have to admit I was taken aback – shaken a bit by what he said – but all the more by the way in which he had said it. There was a fierce, though compassionate certainty in his presence, his style, and his tone. He was clearly a wise elder at the very least, and I felt compelled to fully trust what he said. So I faced that wall, held my right hand out directly in front of me, and walked toward that wall without fear or hesitation. The instant my hand made contact with that seemingly solid wall, it fell! Now I was facing the grand re-opening of what had indeed once been a door, with hinges on both the left and the right where those large double doors had once been. I walked through the opening with a deep sense of awe and excitement, and I was greeted by a banquet room full of friendly people eagerly waiting to honor me for the work I had done.

There are dreams that need to be decoded – those that demand that we dig deeply enough into our own subconscious to decipher the symbols rendered by the energy of the dream. And there are those that are as clear as day, with powerful, straightforward language and imagery that would be missed entirely if we felt the need to dig beneath the clear and obvious meaning offered to us through boldness and beauty that we wake from and remember with startling detail. Neither the lucid dreams we ponder in daylight nor the subconscious dreams that lead us through the night should be dismissed as merely dreams. They are faithful guides and spirited messengers wishing to convey information that could, in fact, prove to be invaluable.

> *"Life begins with the dream and proceeds outward from there."*
> —C.G. JUNG

Nowhere To Go
but the Garden

✳   ✳   ✳

When there's nowhere else to go, I
find a garden. Nearly any garden
will do, when I'm blissfully lost and
lonely enough to reinvent myself.

And when there's no one to go with
me, I go alone; I walk alone toward
the roses – past those towering rows
of cypress pointing upward – always

upward like fertile green arrows
aiming at the sun, the moon, the
stars, and all that can and can't be seen
between them. I walk toward twilight

slowly, taking notice of those white
tea roses climbing up and over a red
brick wall, near that artful iron gate
that never closes. I stand alone near

that three-tiered fountain, watching a
ruby-throated hummingbird taking
a drink from the round marble tier
at the very top. I watch a seagull bathe

in a nearby waterfall, then make my
way along the well-paved path – past
coral bark maples, beyond the olive grove.

I walk past dozens of boulders and
sizeable stones and tell myself – I'm
not one of them! I feel what they cannot…
they never weep, never bleed, nor have their hearts broken.

At the End
of the Week

✳ ✳ ✳

At the end of the week I'm left with a sense of wanting to do better. That's not necessarily a bad thing, nor does it coincide with what I would be inclined to call ideal. I suppose that means I'm in the middle of life, feeling pushed, pulled, touched, and inspired by the grandeur and miracles giving birth to this shifting awareness, offering meaning to my existence along with the continual challenge to take notice of all the splendor I don't want to miss.

I could consult a jumpy compass that belonged to a man who never really found his own true north. I know where to find that questionable compass, though I have little faith or reason to believe it would do any good. It has become a rather impractical artifact by virtue of having been deprived of its magnetic properties. I have a dead man's compass – safe inside its leather case – that has become a sentimental souvenir, for the most part – a memento that takes on a whole new meaning when I find myself marooned on a seemingly tiny island of the mind, feeling slightly less than centered on a poignant and emotional archipelago. That jumpy compass in its leather case is a reminder to me of what we can't rely on. And that is useful – maybe even the metaphorical equivalent of a working compass, a colorful map, and the dusted lens of an intuitive telescope that allows us to see into our future as well as our past.

We need to know what can't be trusted to get us where we truly wish to go. And so, at the end of the week, I was left with a sense of wanting to do better, yearning to do something different – to learn something new and valuable and put it to use in order to give more and give it now! That's what it really comes down to. That's what it's really all about – the giving that permits us to share our gift.

There is this courtyard that I visit from time to time, where an ancient sundial, molded from iron, stands securely upon a pedestal made of stone. There is a lovely archway leading to a modern labyrinthine garden – a magnificent maze that leaves one spellbound while spiraling through this deliberately surrealistic, verdant splendor. I go there to remember the importance of being lost. I go there to walk in circles and come back to the beginning. I go there to get away from the lunatic linear world where lines are drawn to limit and inhibit imagination. I go there to escape the confines of popular preprogrammed perception, urging us to see what isn't there and overlook what is. And I go there because I find it beautiful. Beauty tends to lift us into a higher and better realm, capturing our awareness long enough for us to open up and expand our views of our whole world when we are willing to.

And so, at the end of the week, I was left with a sense of wanting to do better... and now I'm sensing that I have.

Closing Words

※　※　※

As a writer, poet, and impassioned public speaker, it's always and forever about beginnings for me. It's about fresh starts, faithful leaps, and empowering openings. It's about following the robust spirit of free-flowing thought without any absolute certainty as to where it may lead. It requires the willingness to let go and cling to nothing while trading one awareness for another whenever necessary – a perpetual shift in your conscious perception wherein boundaries become bridges, and barriers turn into roads and waterways that lead to landscapes, seascapes, and mindscapes rarely seen.

Any writer worth their salt must commit themselves to beginning after beginning – to each simple yet sacred starting point that has no end that can be known at the outset. Beginnings can be seen and known and realized repeatedly, whereas ends can only be imagined. Endings are illusory as far as I can tell. They are all that remain of the many grand abstractions we felt compelled to wrestle with along the way. They are the high or low notes we hold and devote our breath to near the end of a unique song – the remarkable threading of all those lively remnants artfully woven into the garment of life we wear to cover and/or embellish our own nakedness.

Everyone is naked at the beginning of their lives. I suppose, then, that it must be fitting for us to be naked again near the end that doesn't really end. And if endings are as illusory as I believe them to be, then beginnings must be the essential fantasies we rely on to continue.

Now that you're near the end of this book, you must be closer than ever to a rich and true beginning, not necessarily because of this book or in spite of it, but because beginnings are the fundamental nature of creativity – and creativity is Life!

www.ingramcontent.com/pod-product-compliance
Lightning Source LLC
Chambersburg PA
CBHW051131260626
47170CB00005B/1768